NO ONE'S PERFECT

NO ONE'S PERFECT

by *Betty Carlson*

With illustrations also by the author

GOOD NEWS PUBLISHERS
Westchester, Illinois

Appreciation is extended to the former editor of the
Rockford Morning Star, Mr. John Grimes, and also to
Dr. Paul Vigness ("Lutherans Alert"), Evelyn McClusky
("The Conqueror"), and Mrs. B. W. Adams ("Lutheran
Women" in Australia) for their permission to reprint
some of the material in this book.
—B.C.

Cover Design: Wayne Hanna

Library of Congress Catalog Number 76-17669
ISBN 0-89107-143-1

*To Margaret, Marilyn, and Norval
and anyone in Rockford, Illinois who
remembers a little newspaper column
called "I Love People"*

Contents

Introduction

"Many times I took up my pen to write," said Cervantes, "and many times I put it down, not knowing what to say." I am able to identify with this great Spanish writer, at least, in that aspect of his creativity. He said that he toiled harder over the prologue to *Don Quixote*, than the rest of the book. Introductions are difficult to write, and often disheartening that many readers run past them as if they were infectious.

Please do not skip over this introduction. It is necessary or after a few chapters you are going to sound like two people who have just been to a party. One says, "Who did you say that man was, you know, the one in the yellow shirt, blue trousers, and red socks?" "How should I know," the other person answers. "We were never introduced."

I should like to introduce to you three places and two people. It won't take long. I'll be brief:

L'Abri Fellowship—This is an international community located in a tiny village in the Swiss Alps. It is known as a place where historic, Biblical Christianity is placed in contact with the cultural and intellectual problems of the twentieth century. The work began over twenty years ago when the Francis A. Schaeffer family opened their chalet and their hearts to students wandering about Europe seeking purpose and meaning to life.

Today there are many others who help in the work. Because the L'Abri chalets are always crowded, some people must find their own accommodations, so that they will be nearby to attend lectures, Bible studies, prayer meetings, concerts, or whatever is going on in the community.

Also in the village is Bellevue, a home for children with cerebral palsy. The staff and children are closely knit to those of us who have lived here for many years.

As Edith Schaeffer once said about L'Abri Fellowship, and it is true of Bellevue too, "We have no plan for the work in weeks and years ahead, but we attempt to be sensitive to the Lord's plan day by day. As none of us is perfect, our working together is not perfect either. But there has been an exciting measure of reality in our attempt to follow God's plan for the work." The word "L'Abri" is French and means "The Shelter."

Chalet le Chesalet is one of the homes in the L'Abri community. Living in the small music box chalet are two characters. You may interpret the word as you like.

The one who is called "the musician," sometimes "the Virginian," or "the ardent gardener" is Jane Stuart Smith. Formerly she sang in opera. She is a member of L'Abri Fellowship where she not only continues to sing, but she also teaches the Bible (in several languages), lectures on art, music, and literature, raises chickens, is the soprano soloist for the L'Abri Ensemble, gardens with enthusiasm, and is the hostess of Chesalet.

Also living at Chalet le Chesalet is an independent journalist, "moi," a French word meaning me. That about covers it.

The introductions are over, and it is my sincere prayer that if today is not a good one for you, that some word in this book will help to make it better, or even the best day you have ever had. But if it is a happy day, I hope you let it bubble over to others, like the composer, Joseph Haydn, who was criticized by some of the "religious" people of his day because he was so cheerful. "I cannot help it," he said. "I give forth what is in me. When I think of the Divine Being, my heart is so full of joy that the notes fly off as from a spindle. And as I have a cheerful heart, I am sure God will pardon me if I serve Him cheerfully."

No one's perfect. I hope God will forgive me for trying to write an encouraging, wholesome book in an age when it is the "norm" to be despondent, pessimistic, morally sick, unrestrained, and sensational. I forgot to mention in the "introductions" that one of my eccentricities is that I have never cared to run with the crowd. *Betty Carlson*

1
The Advantages
of Disadvantages

A student once asked his sociology professor to define life. Without hesitating, the teacher replied, "Life is a mysterious force operating mysteriously in a mysterious medium!"

He quickly added, with a smile, "Now you know what life is!"

It is true. We do not know much more about life than that. We know it is. If you are reading these words, you are alive. Nobody has to convince you of that. You have life. I have life. But the important question is,—what are we doing with our lives? Are they counting for something or someone?

On a visit to Edinburgh, some friends and I walked by the house where Sir Walter Scott lived for many years. In his lifetime, his home had been the social center of Scotland. Scott seemed to be a man of leisure and at the disposal of his numerous guests. Only his most intimate friends knew how hard he worked.

Scott did his writing early in the morning, and for the first dozen years or so, he published his works anonymously. He was known as "The Great Unknown." Historians will long remember Sir Walter Scott as the creator of the historical novel. I will always remember him as a noble soul who knew about the "advantages of disadvantages."

People enjoyed being with Scott. He most generally gave the appearance of well-being and ease. His friends and acquaintances really loved him. As one critic said, "Scott was a man free from self-pity." And what was unusual, he had every reason to feel sorry for himself. Infantile paralysis at an early age had left him lame. At the height of his literary career, the publishing house with which he was working, failed. Even though he was not really obliged to pay the debts of the publishing firm, immediately Scott went to work to help pay off these debts.

He overworked, and soon his health gave away. He spent a winter in Italy and then died in the autumn of that year, 1832.

A contemporary of Sir Walter Scott was the poet, Lord Byron. He also was lame, but his infirmity embittered him. He brooded on it until he loathed it. His mind was so fixed on his lameness that much of the color and zest of life were lost to him. One day Scott received a letter from his friend, Lord Byron. "Oh Scott," he said. "I would give all my fame to have your happiness."

I read of a gifted artist and teacher in Germany, a very kind person. Many of his pupils studied with him free of charge. Some of the more sensitive ones would apologize because they could not afford to pay him. He would say to them, "That's all right. Just work very hard."

John Bunyan, a man of little education, was a tinker

(a mender of pots and pans) and a nonconformist minister in Bedford, England. He was arrested for preaching without a license, and in 1660 he was put in jail. He spent most of the next twelve years in prison. Finally he was released in 1672 and by 1675 he was back in jail. It was at this time that he began to write *Pilgrim's Progress*.

It would not seem that this is the best background for developing into a great writer, but *Pilgrim's Progress* is, perhaps, one of the best loved and most famous books in the world.

A Time to Ponder: Many people live from day to day waiting for more perfect conditions, waiting for someone else to help them, waiting for the advantageous moment, but nothing good seems to come to those who sit back and wait. It is important in life to learn how to turn disadvantages into advantages. I have a piece of paper pasted in the fly-leaf of my dictionary. As I am continually opening and shutting the dictionary when at work, I have decided that this is the right place for it. These are my ground rules for writing: Do not expect anything from anyone. Demand much from yourself. Care sincerely for others, hope largely for all (remembering no one's perfect), and pray without ceasing.

"Not slothful in business; fervent in spirit; serving the Lord."

Romans 12:11

2
Live One Day
At A Time

She was only a small child, and she had recently learned to tell time. She felt very important when she was asked to report what time it was. And so one evening after supper, the family was gathered around the dining room table under the kerosene lamp, with the stove in the corner giving off a pleasant heat. Several of the children were playing a game at one end of the table, and at the same time eating hard, crunchy apples and dipping their hands into several bowls of hot buttered popcorn. Their mother, who was seated near the stove, was working on an afghan of many colors, and in between times, she was teaching the two older girls how to braid a rug. The father was reading the Swedish newspaper which was printed in Chicago, and at a certain moment he looked up over his store-bought glasses and said kindly, "Edith, my child, will you please tell me the time?"

The little girl pushed back her chair and ran over to

the grandfather clock and looked up at it in a most earnest way. She reported to her father that the small hand was on nothing, and, oh my, the big hand was also on nothing. "Why, papa," she exclaimed. "It's no time at all!"

There is a part of us that really wishes this was so—that there is no time at all. But those of us who have lived one half of a century or longer are conscious that time moves on even when the hands of the clock point to nothing. If we are going to live the sort of life that has meaning and significance, not only for ourselves, but for others too, we have to come to terms with time.

An ancient philosopher said, "Time is the most valuable thing that a man can spend." And how often we say, about the most important issues in life, as well as lesser things, "All I need is a little more time."

The Scriptures say that to everything there is a season, and a time to every purpose under the sun. The time of the Swiss autumn crocus has recently come and gone in the fields of our tiny village. But before the pale, purple flowers withered and died, they waved their farewell, like tiny flags on a parade ground heralding the next special event in God's annual fall festival.

It is as certain as the forsythia and weeping willow trees explode their brightness on the hillside each Spring before the dignified blue iris come for their visit, and as sure as red raspberries always come after the plump strawberries, so the fields of autumn crocus are always followed by the sound of the Swiss cowbells.

One day last fall as I was sitting on the balcony, thinking a little, writing less, and mostly wondering, a parade of handsome Swiss cows passed by on the path below, coming down from the Alpine pastures to return to the village barns for the winter. Each cow has her own bell. Some of them so large you wonder how the cows can hold up their heads, but our Swiss neighbors tell us that the cows are very proud of their bells. Those at the head of the parade have the largest bells.

The clear, warm air was ringing with music, and the beauty of the trees in their autumn finery, the neatness of Switzerland, fresh snow on the mountain peaks, and the sweet corn almost ready to pick... It was one of those moments you wish you could hold on to forever. And I experienced that most bewildering of all human emotions,—great joy and deep sadness at the same time.

Joy because of God's wondrous gift of life, and tears because a part of your mind knows your earthly life is not going on forever. That is when the words of Scripture mean the most: "God will take care of your tomorrow too." Christ's message to those of us who believe in Him is: "Live one day at a time."

And in a few verses preceeding this are these special words: "Don't worry about things. If God cares so wonderfully for flowers that are here today and gone tomorrow, won't He more surely care for you?" Let me repeat the last verse: "So don't be anxious about tomorrow. God will take care of your tormorrow too. Live one day at a time."

Ecclesiastes 3:1
Matthew 6:25, 30, 34 (Living Bible)

A Time to Ponder: It is not *all* joy having cows grazing in the field next to your fence. The musician looked out the window one beautiful Spring morning and saw the contented-looking creatures eating the leaves and buds from our pear trees. Out she rushed making quite a commotion, but it was too late. They had enjoyed a substantial meal. We had a rather slim harvest of pears that year.

In thinking about time, surely one of the favorite

Swiss cows lunching
on Chesalet pear blossoms

verses among believers is in Psalm 90. "So teach us to number our days, that we may apply our hearts unto wisdom." And we do pray, that in the days and years we have ahead, dear Saviour, we will live closely to You so the beauty of the LORD our Lord will be upon us and radiate from us.

One of my editors, who does radiate the beauty and wonder of the Christian faith, wrote on his 80th birthday, "I was very amused to see Dr. Taylor's translation of Psalm 90; verse 10, 'Seventy years are given to us! And some may even live to eighty.' "

When you have time,—no, that is a poor way to use the great gift of time: TAKE time to read and pray through Matthew, chapter six and Psalm 90. Be thankful for the different translations available to us today which help to make the Bible come alive.

Psalm 90, verse 12 (King James)
verse 10 (Living Bible)

3
No One's Perfect

Verdi's opera "La Traviata" was a failure when it was first performed. Even though the singers chosen for the lead roles were the best of the day, everything went wrong. The tenor had a cold and sang in a hoarse, almost inaudible voice. The soprano, who played the part of the delicate, sickly heroine, was one of the stoutest ladies on or off the stage, and very healthy and loud.

At the beginning of the Third Act when the doctor declares that consumption has wasted away the "frail, young lady" and she cannot live more than a few hours, the audience was thrown into a spasm of laughter, a state very different from that necessary to appreciate the tragic moment!

Who doesn't have days like that when everything goes wrong, when we become overwhelmingly conscious of our frailty and imperfection. At those times it is good to remember this is not our world. The earth is the Lord's. "You cannot stir a flower without troubling a star." And so the sooner we learn to walk closely with God who is in charge and who does not change, the happier we will be.

In life we have the good and the bad, the up and down, laughter and tears, and confusion, change, and unending interruptions. In the midst of it all, it is balm in Gilead to hear the psalmist say: "I said to Jehovah, 'Thou art my LORD; I have no good beside Thee' ... In Thy presence is fulness of joy." These words can sound faraway to our ears so accustomed to bad news, but it is exactly what the Christian faith is about. I too can say, "You are my LORD; I have no good beyond You, and in Your presence is fulness of joy," because of Christ's finished work on the cross.

Obviously no one has "fulness of joy" every moment of every day, and the explanation involves a very small word with far-reaching consequences and penetrating depths. The word is sin. Because the concept of sin is highly out of favor today does not change its original meaning. As Luther once said concerning the whole Bible: "The objectivity and certainty of the Word remain even if it isn't believed."

Authentic Christians keep in mind the truth that we live in a fallen world. Sin is sin, and it has altered all of us. Everyone is out of step, including myself. There is no perfection anywhere. Everything human is marred. If we disregard this basic truth, we become phony Christians who live out our lives in misery, romantically demanding from others (as well as ourselves) more than we can be. We all fall short of God's moral excellence.

In the small village where I live in Switzerland, we hear it over and over, "No one is perfect." NO ONE IS PERFECT. No, not one. When I first heard this it seemed like such an obvious thing to say. Why keep repeating it? But as I have been examining this proposition for many years now, it has finally impressed my imperfect mind that it is a true and right statement and not one bit obvious. Over and over in life we tend to forget that no one's perfect.

Why do we have so much trouble in life? particularly with other people?—and more particularly with the culprit known as myself? It is fairly understandable why the sparks fly among people who do not give even a tiny nod to the One who died to save sinners, but why are we Christians involved in fireworks of our own so much of the time?

If you stop and think about it, over and over in life we set up standards which are impossible to reach, and equally impossible to maintain, forgetting completely that no one is perfect. It helps to explain why we are despondent, out of sorts, critical, mean, and even cruel, not only to others, but to ourselves. We curl our lips (the bad characters in Dickens' novels are always curling their lips) and sneer, "She shouldn't dress like that." "Did you see Jim last night, louder than ever." And there is this familiar refrain, "I'm planning to lose 50 pounds beginning next week" (and there is always some relative or friend nearby, who is as thin as a piece of string, to add, "You surely ought to!") ... etc., etc...

We are not perfect, and the Word of God does not demand perfection from us. The perfection we do have is found in Christ Jesus when we believe in Him. This gives us the privilege, any time of the day or night to speak as comfortably and personally to God as the shepherd boy who became a king addressed his Lord: "The LORD is my shepherd; I shall not want. He maketh me to lie down in green pastures: he leadeth me beside the still waters. He restoreth my soul: he leadeth me in the paths of righteousness for his name's sake..."

Psalm 16:2 and 11 (Berkeley)
Psalm 23:1-3

A Time to Ponder: Read and think through Psalms 16 and 23. Compare the difference between the unbeliever in the Living God ("Their sorrows shall be multiplied that hasten after another god," Psalm 16:4) and the believer ("Surely goodness and mercy shall follow me all the days of my life: and I will dwell in the house of the Lord forever," Psalm 23:6). No one is perfect, but it is all gain to set the LORD always before us and walk with Him.

Each time the wise man told the old grouch to bring into the one room hut one of the farm animals. Conditions became worse and worse as three goats, seven chickens, two lambs, and an important-acting pig were brought inside, one by one. There was scarcely room to sit by the fire and smoke a pipe. The old man was beside himself with rage.

In desperation, he again went to the wise man, who told the peasant that he should now start removing the animals from the hut, in the same order in which he had brought them in...

By the end of two weeks when the last animal was put outside, the old man made a wonderful discovery. He found out that their one room hut was not as small as he thought it was, and that there *was* plenty of room for the baby to crawl, the women to cook and spin, and the two men to sit by the fire and smoke their pipes.

Obviously, this is a story that is pre-women's liberation, but it illustrates a point. It is somewhat the same with trouble. We think we have more burdens than we can bear, and then some really tragic things occur, and we wonder at our shortsightedness in not appreciating life when we had it so good. As an elderly man wrote, "I am eighty and find life very difficult not being able to get about much. But praise the Lord, "I can 'crawl about' with a stick and I still have my eyesight."

Short Prayer: O God, You know my frequent downsittings and occasional uprisings. Forgive me for failing to be thankful this day for the truly grand things in life—that You really do exist, that You gave us the Bible that we might know You, that You sent Your Son to die for people like us, and that He arose from the dead and is now seated at God's right hand. O teach us to set our affections on things above, not on the changing, shifting things of this world. Help us to eliminate our tiresome complaining about "little" things when there are such benefits in praising and giving thanks for all Your goodness to us. We pray in the name of our Saviour. Amen.

A Time to Ponder: A friend advised an unhappy, middle-aged father to take his troubles to the Lord. "Fine," he complained, "I do, but so many of my troubles come from *other* people!" That sounds simple, but actually it is profound. Shakespeare spent the greater part of his life developing the theme: Stability in life depends on everyone's observing his proper degree in it. Most Christians know that the answer to the enormous problem of getting along with other people is to love them, but it is the rare person who gets beneath the surface of the command "to love," and understands what it really means. It sounds like the following observation could have been made by the wise man we read about: "To love one's neighbor does not at all mean making out that he is a nice fellow when he is not; we are only asked to love our neighbors as we love ourselves, and what is very lovable in any of us?"

One can think about that a *long* time.

5
Mercy Begins at Home

In the novel, *Bleak House*, by Charles Dickens, Esther, an orphan and a likable young lady, spends a night in the home of Mr. and Mrs. Jellyby. The gentleman who arranges the visit assumes that Esther has heard of her famous hostess, but Esther humbly admits she knows nothing whatever about Mrs. Jellyby.

" 'Indeed! Mrs. Jellyby,' said Mr. Kinge, standing with his back to the fire, and casting his eyes over the dusty hearthrug as if it were Mrs. Jellyby's biography, 'is a lady of very remarkable strength of character, who devotes herself entirely to the public... At present she is devoted to the subject of Africa; with a view to the general cultivation of the coffee berry—*and* the natives.' "

Then follows an hilarious, satirical account of the great lady's home. It is disorganized, dirty, and cluttered with untidy, neglected children. Esther observes that Mrs. Jellyby has handsome eyes, though they had a curious habit of seeming to look way off. Her hair was naturally attractive, but she was much too occupied with Africa to brush it, and Esther couldn't help noticing that her dress didn't "meet up the back."

For dinner they were served a fine codfish, a piece of beef, a dish of cutlets, and a Yorkshire pudding, an excellent meal, excepting it was almost raw. Among the other guests at the table was a gentleman whom Esther had not met. As she was puzzling who he was, it came to her. It must be Mrs. Jellyby's husband. He seemed to be on the verge of saying something several times, he even opened his mouth once, but nothing came out. However, as Esther quietly observed to herself, his remarks were not greatly missed as there was an intense conversation going on between Mrs. Jellyby and an admirer about African coffee berries—and natives. As they spoke, important letters were passed between them and read outloud. Later Esther told some friends, "At one time four envelopes fell in the gravy."

In the evening after dinner, Mr. Jellyby slumped in a corner with his head against the wall, as if he were subject to low spirits, while his wife became more lively as the evening went on. She sat in a "nest of waste paper," drinking endless cups of coffee, and discussing the Brotherhood of Humanity. At intervals when a brilliant idea would come upon her, she would stop to dictate a letter to her eldest daughter...

It is not surprising to learn that Mrs. Jellyby soon tires of cultivating African coffee berries and natives, and with scarcely a glance to see how the family is getting along, she turns her passionate nature to women's rights. As a friend of mine, a thoughtful and contented wife and mother, commented (she too has been reading Dickens),

"*Anything* to keep from having to clean up the house, care for her children and husband, and do something for the neighbors and relatives!"

It is interesting (and sad) to note how the Mrs. Jelly-bys of the world continue to be stunned when their daughters become alcoholics, their sons escape into drugs, and the husbands are never heard of again,—"I taught them to love humanity, and *this* is the thanks I get." Perhaps it could be said, that works without faith can destroy a family.

In the story of the Good Samaritan, Jesus asked the lawyer, who was questioning Him about eternal salvation, "Which of these three, do you think, proved himself a neighbor to him who fell among the robbers?" He answered, "The one who showed pity and mercy to him." Jesus said, "Go and do likewise."

Luke 10:36, 37 (Amplified Bible)

A Time to Ponder: A child of ten (or so) once said to her mother, "I wish there was something for me to do." The mother replied, "I can find you plenty of jobs." "Oh," the young girl quickly answered, "I don't mean ordinary things like *that!*"

Happiness is discovering that the best way to serve God is to do the small, ordinary task right at hand, or around the corner, and trust the Lord that He can hold His own in far away places. O, yes, of course, there are those called for special works, to foreign countries, etc., but they will make singularly unsatisfactory missionaries if they arrive at their post with stars in their eyes and no calluses on their hands, or, at least, the willingness to develop a few.

A friend, who is now a missionary in France, spent several years at L'Abri Fellowship mostly scrubbing floors, cleaning bathrooms, washing stacks of dishes, answering the telephone, and other necessary chores. She told me the other day that it was the best preparation she could have had for her present work. In her unassuming, cheerful way she shared with me a French expression, which goes something like this: "The authentic Christian does not seek to do extraordinary things, but to do extraordinarily well the ordinary thing."

"Dear Lord, Please help us to walk worthy of our calling. May others know we are Christians by what we do."

Read Romans, Chapter 12 as a guide to how we are to live.

6
A Friend Like Titus

Paul wrote about one of his difficult times in life: "As we reached Macedonia,—there was trouble at every turn, wranglings outside of me and fears within me. But God, the Encourager of the downhearted, did console us by the arrival of Titus..."

At least two or three letters arrive at our little house in Switzerland every week. They are from a friend in Virginia. How she does it, I really do not know, because our friend is almost blind and deaf, but she keeps us informed about everything. Yes, everything. Not always perfectly accurate, but, on the other hand, a lot more correct than much of the news I receive. She has a special lens which fits on her glasses which gives her enough sight to read and write,—not much, but enough for someone as persevering as Anne. Also she is greatly helped by her mother who forms the letters in her hand to explain something difficult. Because of her handicaps, her way of expressing herself is quaint and sometimes highly entertaining. May I share a few excerpts from these special letters?

She always begins with the hope that "both of you are well. We are fine," usually followed by a weather report—"It is hot and sunny here today. It cooled here all day yesterday and last night sleeps very comfortable. It cooled last Sat. nite too. Many, many hundred thanks a million for the beautiful Swiss musical. This is making me too happy. I love Switzerland and the cows very much."

In many letters we receive clippings pertaining to births, deaths, marriages, etc., thus she continued,

"I'm enclosing this obituary article for you today in case you might have known her. The cause of death was autopsy. We felt very sadly. Goodbye, I will write again soon."

I am happy to say that we did not know the person who died of autopsy.

Another point that must be explained about Anne, is that she is a celebrator. She loves to give and receive. She not only remembers us at Easter, Valentine's Day, birthdays, Christmas, and other holidays, but she has added several in our families as recipients of her bountifulness too. We all have a strenuous time trying to keep even!

There is no child who joys in Christmas more than Anne. She looks forward to it months ahead, and dies a little each year when it is over. After last Christmas she wrote,

"I am wishing you a very Happy New Year. Christmas just came, then has gone forever. I took my Christmas decorations off my living room last Friday night and Saturday. I cleaned up the room Monday. I will not return same old decorations again next Christmas. I want something new to decorate."

Weather report again:

"It is damp and hot here. Have you had any deep snow up there yet? I hope every one in the Alps are well. Give them all my love."

Anne loves to go shopping:

"Mother and I went on shopping yesterday. We ate good dinner at Woolworth Store of baked beans, hot dogs, brown bread and butter, vanilla milk shake and my favorite strawberry short cake with whipped cream all over. We enjoyed the shopping very much."

"Yes thank you, thank you. I had a very nice birthday. I got 30 birthday cards, several nice checks, 22 gifts, and three lovely real flowers. I was very surprised to get three lovely flowers. That made me so bright and smiling. Mother bought me a new pair of gray Puppy Hush shoes from Bush and Flora Shoe Company. They was my birthday present from my beloved sweet mother. I am wearing them now, very soft, like cats' paws. I will send a picture of me in them."

During the oil crisis, Anne wrote,

"I have an idea as I could help you. It is too hard about gasoline and fuel oil when people needs to travel and take vacations, etc., and also for your concert tour too. You better buy some gallons of gasoline, then pour them into a big tank where it can be laid in your lawn up there. Please let me know if this works."

Then one day we had a letter telling about her new dentures. "Too beautiful," she described them and also promised to send a picture.

As mentioned, she loves sending and receiving presents. She wrote once, "Hoping this gift of check finds you joyous and happiness thinking of me a lot." It was Paul who wrote about another of his beloved friends, Timothy, "I remember you night and day in my prayers." We feel the same about Anne.

As you have heard mentioned in this book that no one's perfect, it turned out that we missed sending a

34

present for Anne's 50th birthday. We felt horrid, and quickly mailed off a small check with a big apology. You might know, she loves belated presents!

"Oh, very much bigger, bigger surprise to find a beautiful check of $10.00 and a wonderful funny birthday card that was my belated birthday present. These arrived to me safely today at 11 o'clock. I just told my dear Lord Jesus Christ and His Heavenly Father about your kindness after I opened it. I thanked Him very much for His wondrous gift. Many, many hundred thanks a million."

Who wouldn't enjoy having a friend like Anne whose enthusiasm knows no limits. We know we are not worthy of such love, and can only say what Paul said about his friends who cared for him, "I thank my God upon every remembrance of you."

II Corinthians 7:5, 6 (Berkeley)

II Timothy 1:3

Philippians 1:3

A Time to Ponder: Minding one's own business is difficult to do. The greater part of humanity is so taken up with correcting and criticizing and straightening out the lives of others, they never get on with living their own lives. As I was reading yesterday, in the Living Bible, "A constant dripping on a rainy day and a cranky woman are much alike! You can no more stop her complaints than you can stop the wind or hold onto anything with oil-slick hands." And a whining child or fault-finding man are equally dampening. I believe that is why Paul appreciated Titus. He came as an encourager at a time when the apostle was downhearted and troubled.

Life is hard enough for all of us (but as Sydney Harris once said, "When I hear somebody sigh, 'Life is hard,' I am always tempted to ask, 'Compared to what?' "), but the essential thing is to get on with our own lives. That is why Anne is a special friend—she is supremely living her own life, not one bit interested in straightening out the lives of her friends. But she is cheerfully thankful to God they exist and devoted to the cause of making them glad they are alive too. One of her letters recently ended on this high note, "You and Jane are my very best and the world's most popular friends." I had been in a letter writing slump, but that sent me to my desk determined to write twenty-one "bright and smiling" letters which I knew I should write, but hadn't.

Maybe you do not have a Titus in your life to encourage you, but if you know the Lord Jesus Christ as your Saviour, you have a Friend who is better than all earthly friends, and if you ask Him, He not only can send you a friend, but He can help you to be a Titus to someone who needs your love and encouragement. As it says in Proverbs, "A man that hath friends must shew himself friendly: and there is a friend that sticketh closer than a brother."

Anne's most recent letter had this P.S.—"Ten more months until Christmas. I keep thinking about Christmas often."

Proverbs 27:15 (Living Bible)
Proverbs 18:24

Dear Lord, Help me to think about Christmas more often too. May I truly understand that the birth of Christ, His death and resurrection have something to do with my life right now. Give me the courage to live for You, and even if many of the things I do go unnoticed, may I have deep joy in knowing I am doing it unto You. Thank You, dear Lord, for imparting to my heart, the blessings of heaven. In the name of Jesus I pray. Amen.

7
"Words Spoken in Season"

One day the editor of a new children's magazine asked A. A. Milne to write some verse. Later he wrote, "I said that I didn't and couldn't, it wasn't my line. As it turned out, it was."

If Milne were alive today, he would be astonished how far Pooh and Piglet have gone,—and don't forget Eyeore. They are familiar figures to TV audiences, they dance and stump across stages all over the world, children carry them to bed every night, and Milne's four books have sold millions of copies in I don't know how many languages.

In one way this success story that "didn't and couldn't" seem possible, but was, brings to my mind the great missionary to China, Matthew Yates. As a young boy helping on his father's prosperous farm in North Carolina about one century and a half ago,— while feeding the cattle, swinging an axe, or hunting wild turkey or partridge, Matthew never dreamed he would someday go to the Orient, and even more,—that he would be the first missionary to go to a foreign land from his state.

Nor could he imagine that he, a shy, quiet person, a slow student (one of his friends at Wake Forest College remembered him as a plodder) would one day become so proficient in speaking Chinese that his Shanghai friends used to say, "Yates is no foreigner; he is a Chinaman with his queue cut off."

This impossible-to-learn language has 44,700 characters in the standard dictionary, and what is more difficult than mere vocabulary are the 700 distinct sounds, to each of which is attached a sort of musical scale. The all-important thing is the tone. For example, a man is "a man" only when the proper tone is given. If a speaker is slightly off tune, a man easily becomes a carrot or a nightingale. To give a tiny glimpse of the complexity of the Chinese language the same word may mean elephant, grasshopper, mechanic, or pickle, according to the tone. Some of the first sermons new missionaries attempt in this amazing language are high comedy.

There were several reasons why Dr. Yates excelled in the spoken language of Chinese. He had a good musical ear, a flexible voice and an acute sense of hearing, and though he was not a brilliant student in college, he was always thorough and a perseverer. Then there were two other reasons to help explain his exceptional attainments. He was threatened with the loss of his eyesight which forced him out into the streets of Shanghai to mingle with the people and to imitate their way of speaking.

But the most important reason Matthew Yates excelled, not only in speaking the Chinese language, but as a missionary, was his genuine dependence upon God. His faith was not the super-zeal and franticness of some in religious work who give the impression that missionaries are different from other people.

His letters from China are the most relaxed, happy, funny, penetratingly true missionary observations I have had the privilege to read. Here is one brief sample before we return to his boyhood days down on the farm in North Carolina. He is telling of one of their first excursions into the interior near Shanghai, traveling by boat: "By some means, the news of our coming went ahead of us, and when we approached a village we found the banks of the canal and the fine stone bridges crowded with gazers; men, women, and children.

"We were not long in finding out that the wisest policy, to avoid being stoned out, was to stand on the bow of the boat, so that they could have a full-length view. What was more satisfactory was to stop the boat and go on shore, where all could have the full gratification of a near approach to and a thorough examination of the Western man, who was supposed to be hairy, like a horse."

"Under these circumstances, it was necessary to command the crowd; and the only way to do this was to speak to them—get the floor and keep it—till I was ready to return to my boat, and then leave immediately."

"In carrying out this expedient, to preserve order and prevent a riot, I addressed myself to the more intelligent and thoughtful looking of the spectators in front of me; while at my sides and back as many as could get to me were deeply interested in examining my clothes and pulling up the legs of my trousers to see if my legs were really covered with hair like the legs of a horse."

"While thus engaged, they were warned by their friends of the danger of being kicked. I have heard them reply to this warning, 'Why, he is not like a horse at all; his skin is whiter and smoother than ours.' They had an impression, too, that a foreigner's legs were stiff, having no knee joints. One examination by a dozen persons was sufficient to inform and satisfy a town or a large region of country."

In telling of his boyhood days, Matthew Yates said,

"My father delighted in keeping open-house for preachers ... I remember one putting his hand on my head and saying, 'May the Lord make a preacher of him.' At some time subsequent to this, my father's friend asked me if I ever prayed; to which I replied that I did not know how to pray. He looked kindly at me, as I held his horse to mount, and said, 'I will tell you, "God be merciful to me, a sinner."' This short prayer has remained with me from that day to the present time," wrote Dr. Yates. "It was the first intimation I ever had that I was a sinner."

At still another time the kind, older preacher asked Yates if he had prayed the prayer he had taught him. The future missionary replied that he had not, because he did not know where to pray. And the friend said, "Go into the woods where none can hear you. God is everywhere."

The great missionary, Dr. Matthew Yates, said later in his life, "Those were 'words spoken in season.' I was quite young, but what he said gave direction to my whole life."

We too, wherever we are in life, must find a quiet spot for prayer. Not many of us today have solitary woods within walking distance where we can find our secret place to commune with God, but woods or no woods, if our Christian lives are going to have depth, we must establish the habit of times alone with God.

I recall reading about a busy mother with many children who solved her need for solitude in a simple, direct way. When things would get beyond her, she would sit down where she was, throw her apron over her head and this was the signal, "Quiet, mother is praying."

And pray she did, and those in her family grew up thanking God for the benefits which crown the lives of those who have had a praying mother.

It takes courage to pray. Sometimes it is impossible to find the quiet spot, and we must pray in front of others. To encourage someone struggling with this problem, let me tell you another true story: It involves a young man from a missionary family. He had heard and seen much of Christianity in his life, but still was not convinced for himself of the necessity of a deeper commitment to God, until in college he saw his roommate, from a very different background than his, get on his knees night after night and pray to the Living God. Then one night the two young men began praying together.

Dare to pray in a crowded restaurant or in front of guests in your own home or in a college dormitory,— not self-righteously, but because it is right to show others that we are truly thankful people. "O give thanks unto the LORD, for He is good: for His mercy endureth for ever. Let the redeemed of the LORD say so..."

But if you cannot (or have not) ever prayed before other people, do not feel badly. I know a lady beloved by her family and friends and known in her church and community for her goodness and gentleness. Never in her entire life has she prayed out loud, but one would never doubt that there is a genuine prayer life going on behind the scene. Once she said, "I have to tell you I had a dream last night. Everyone was asked to pray. I didn't say a word. Someone whispered, 'Alice, you can say, Thank You, dear LORD.' That was all, but I'll always remember to say, 'Thank You, dear LORD.' "

The important thing about prayer is to pray. Where

and when are the details, but if we do not pray, we will live thin, selfish, sad lives with no spiritual fruit. "Man looks on the outward appearance, but the LORD looks on the heart."

Psalm 107:1, 2
I Samuel 16:7 (Berkeley)

A Time to Ponder: Read through some of the great prayers in the Bible. For example, David's prayer in II Samuel 7:18-29 when God denied him the privilege of building the temple. Or Jonah's amazing prayer from the belly of the fish: Jonah, Chapter 2. Or Paul's prayer for the church and for you and me: Ephesians 3:14-21.

When the need arises, pray through one of these prayers word for word thinking of your own life, your own problems, your own needs.

"LORD, teach me to pray, and thank You, dear LORD."

Suddenly a crowd poured out of several doors, and the sidewalk and street filled with people. No longer did I see individuals, only people, all coming from a destination and going to a destination. Abruptly a car squeezed into the parking place in front of me. In the maneuvering the driver banged against my fender. Out of the low sports' car climbed a middle-aged man, impeccably dressed with a hard, mean look on his face. He slammed the door of his car, looked carelessly at his fender to see if it had been scratched, and walked quickly to the newspaper stand.

The lady crouching in the other bucket seat of the Italian racer made an obscene gesture at the retreating man. Her face was more dissipated than his. In the short interval he was away, she smoked two cigarettes and with such nervous, restless gestures, it made me tense to watch, but I couldn't take my eyes away.

When the man returned, he opened the door, threw some papers on the seat, slammed the door, and went across the street toward the other newsstand. She picked up one of the papers and read something on the back page. I could clearly see the name of the paper through our two windshields. It was a scandal sheet which has recently been published in Zurich and has had a phenomenal success in Switzerland. Soon the man came back, threw another bunch of papers and magazines in the lap of the lady (it is just as well I could not hear what she said), and off they roared.

People, only an ordinary crowd of people, coming and going in front of a busy railroad station. People, made in the image of God, some (perhaps many) not in fellowship with God for various reasons. As the Scriptures say, "All have fallen short..." No one is perfect. No not one. And when you sit and look at people and try to see yourself in the crowd too (I won't tell you what I thought when the man banged my car), it is not hard to believe that we have all fallen short of the glory of God. No wonder we lose confidence in ourselves now and then when we see how mean and small we are. As a young lady wrote to me recently, "It's hard for me to admit how really self-centered I am. It's so easy to put on the appearance of being a nice, sweet, polite person, and people complimenting me on this and that, never realizing how ugly I am on the inside."

But do not let anyone tell you the story stops there. There is more, much more, for those who take time to consider the hope which is set before those who believe God. "He hath made us accepted in the beloved," or in another translation: "... We belong to His dearly beloved Son." Still another way of saying the same great truth: "He planned, in His purpose of love, that we should be adopted as His own children through Jesus Christ—that we might learn to praise that glorious generosity of His which has made us welcome in the everlasting love He bears toward the Son."

I did not get to tell the people at the railroad station, but maybe there is someone reading this book who needs to know that they are accepted, that they belong, and that they are welcome to a better way of living that involves now and all of eternity. I do not know about you, but I cherish knowing that I belong, that I am accepted, and that God welcomes even me if I come to Him according to His way.

People, coming and going; it is no small thing to know you are welcome at the other end.

Ephesians 1:6
Ephesians 1:6 (Living Bible)
Ephesians 1:4, 6 (Phillips)

A Time to Ponder: The Christian faith is personal. God is concerned about our destiny. So concerned that He sent His only Son to die on a cross that you and I might

45

9
Wisdom or Gold

"How much better is wisdom than gold, and understanding than silver." A wise proverb taken each day as one enjoys biting into a freshly picked apple might not only keep the doctor away, but also "the roaring lion," Satan. If we read too many headlines and stare too long at television the whole world begins to look like the worst of some of the expressionistic paintings, and we lose the sense of the sovereignty of God. No one can fathom the depths of His understanding, His ways with nations and individuals. And the mystery of mysteries, He is (in His timing) working all things together for good for those who love Him and are called according to His designs and purposes.

How much better is wisdom than gold, and yet I do not have to tell you that the majority of people live, and have lived since the beginning of time, as if the proverb read: "How much better is gold than wisdom."

A friend and I had some of our nieces and nephews

out for lunch one day, and an exciting conversation was taking place about what we all liked best in the world. When the youngest finally had his chance to say something, he flung out his arms and said loudly, "Do you know what I like best in the world?" All eyes focused on him. Rubbing his hands together, and blinking his eyes, he shouted, "MONEY! That's what I like best!" He was either eight or ten years old. I forget now.

It is difficult to get a balanced attitude about money. The best prayer I know on the subject is also in Proverbs: "O God,—give me neither poverty nor riches! Give me just enough to satisfy my needs! For if I grow rich, I may become content without God. And if I am too poor, I may steal, and thus insult God's holy name."

Anyone of us can think of people with wealth who give the outer appearance of well-being. They look as prosperous and handsome as models in a fashion magazine, and their wrinkle-free faces seem to laugh easily; but God is not in their vocabulary, other than as a curse word. A prosperous person who has never thanked His Creator for all that has been given to him, quickly becomes a mocker of God. There is a reason that the Scriptures teach that God sets Himself against the proud and haughty, but gives grace to the lowly, those of an humble mind.

Pastors and their families (up until recently, at least) have seldom had the reputation for having to sleep upon their bags of gold, but the sincere, good ones among them have not been overly disturbed. I believe it is related to their understanding Proverbs 16:16 ("Wisdom is better than gold, and understanding than silver.")—

In the home of the Bronte sisters, which was located on the mist-covered moors of Yorkshire in England, there were few rugs on the floors and no curtains at the windows (their mother had died leaving the father with six small children), but the sparsely furnished manse was filled with books, good books, as many preachers' homes are.

There was such an emphasis on learning in the Bronte home that the room which the children occupied during the day was not called the nursery, nor even the schoolroom, but the *study*. (It would be interesting to find out how many great men and women were born and raised in the homes of clergymen. To mention only a few,—Coleridge, Lewis Carroll, Tennyson, Addision, Jane Austen, Linnaeus, Van Gogh, Matthew Arnold, John and Charles Wesley, and, of course, the Bronte sisters, Charlotte, Emily, and Anne, whose remarkable books are still widely read.)

May more of us Christians be challenged to rise above the low and ugly standards which are set before us in art, music, literature, and television, and turn to the God of all beauty, wisdom, and wonder, Who offers to those who acknowledge Him the best that there is in this world and the one to come. When words are twisted to say the opposite of what is true, we should not be surprised that the results are moral offensiveness, dissatisfaction, and ultimately, lostness.

In spite of the fact that Charlotte Bronte read widely, the only reading which made a strong mark on her works, particularly, the wonderful book *Jane Eyre*, were these,—Shakespeare, the essayists and political writers of the 18th century, Bunyan, Sir Walter Scott, Byron, and the Bible. She was asked once what was the best book in the world. She answered, "The Bible."

Proverbs 16:16 (Living Bible)
Proverbs 30:7-9 (Living Bible)

A Time to Ponder: The life of Charlotte Bronte is sad. Her mother died when she was only five and she and the other children in the family came under the care of the father who was "somewhat eccentric." Later an aunt came and helped with the children. She and two sisters attended the Clergy Daughters' School at Cowan Bridge. There they were subjected to such hardships that the two older sisters became ill and died. The favorite in the family was their brother, Branwell. He became a ne'er-do-well and alcoholic. Charlotte married at the age of 38, and died the year after.

From that imperfect setting and limited experience in the world she wrote several books and experienced recognition as a successful writer because of her novel, *Jane Eyre*. It is still popular today, and its firm moral tone and Christian base is like drinking cool water after a long walk in a barren land.... It can be said about Charlotte Bronte: "This is the victory that overcometh the world, even our faith."

I John 5:4

10
"Domani Ancora"

In Milan, Italy lives a delightful lady. This beloved friend has lived through wars, illnesses, multiplied anxieties, loss of fortune, death of loved ones, hunger, and fear. And yet she has arrived by "reason of strength to fourscore years" and more,—still able to smile, still trusting God, and still caring for other people.

She is full of simple, excellent remedies for all manner of ailments common to frail mankind (you immediately feel healthier talking to her), and no one tells a humorous story better than she does on the theme, "No one is perfect in Italy either." Signora Rolandi is the sort of comfortable, stimulating person you love to visit, and on more than one occasion we have driven through deep snow over the Alps between Switzerland and Italy to pay a brief visit to our friend.

For a number of years she used to visit us every summer. It was shortly after we bought our first chickens *and* were getting more and more involved with the care and feeding of L'Abri guests. She wrote that she would come and see us, only under the following conditions:—that we would allow her to fix all the meals, do the dishes, mend, scrub, wash, iron, and help with the chickens. We wired: "Come immediately and do as you please."

The secret to her strength, her peace, her joy, and her flair for living, can be expressed in two Italian words, "Domani ancora." It simply means, "Tomorrow is another day." Years ago Signora learned to say, "Domani ancora," whenever tragedy or even some little but pesky thing arrived. It is actually a shortened version of Psalm 30, that great song of consolation to those with broken hearts: "Weeping may endure for a night, but joy comes in the morning." Signora explains that sometimes the word, night, may mean many nights, but never mind, you look out the window one morning and the sun is shining.

In a poem by Emily Dickenson, we hear these words:

"The soul has bandaged moments
  When too appalled to stir ..."

and then, in the same poem she tried to express the wonder of joy coming again:

"The soul has moments of escape,
  When, bursting all the doors,
She dances like a bomb abroad,
  And swings upon the hours."

The world, the flesh, and Satan do not control the Christian who makes the effort to burst open the door of self-centeredness, and whose heart is tender and open, not only to God, but to people. I was reading recently that there are (supposedly) two major reasons why people shed tears. One is self-pity, and the other, gratitude. We do grieve about our own mortality, and why shouldn't we? We all have an inner awareness of what John Donne tried to express. Ask not "for whom the bell tolls; it tolls for thee." But I can easily think of 101 other reasons for tears that are not self-pity. There is a gallantry, a beauty, in the way people stand together in the "bandaged moments," particularly, if we have Christian friends and neighbors.

But the *wonder* of the light, happy hours, the times of joy, when in gratitude we shed tears. Here are the dancing moments in life. "Domani ancora" is important to remember. No matter how impossible it might seem today, there are good days ahead for God's people.

A person whose wisdom I respect once said, "If there is nothing else for me to rejoice in right now, the Lord tells me to be joyful in Him."

To discover for one's self how near God is, is one of the delights of real faith. "He that dwelleth in the secret place of the most High shall abide under the shadow of the Almighty... When he calls upon Me, I will answer him; I will be with him in trouble."

Linnaeus, the eminent Swedish naturalist, who established the modern method of naming plants and animals, had inscribed over the door of his lecture room: "Live innocently: God is here."

"Do you not know, have you not heard? The LORD is the everlasting God, the Creator of the ends of the earth; He never faints or grows weary; His wisdom is unsearchable."

During the time Dr. Matthew Yates was a missionary in China, he lived through several rebellions. One time, because of uprisings, he was shut off from the rest of the world for eighteen months. It was during this period of danger and forced inaction that he made good progress in the Shanghai dialect... It is up to us to ask God to show us how to turn our times of waiting into useful hours; and I say this respectfully, knowing how impatient I am. We might not feel like going on, but no Christian has to go on alone. "He imparts vigor to the fainting, and to those who have no might He increases strength. Even youths shall faint and grow weary, and young men go down exhausted; but they that wait upon the LORD shall renew their strength. They shall mount up with wings like eagles; they shall run and not be weary; they shall walk and not faint."

Psalm 30:5 (Amplified)
Psalm 91:1, 15
Isaiah 40:28-31 (B)

A Time to Ponder: While reading Lamentations 3:21-26, think about Jeremiah. In his lifetime he experienced rejection from his neighbors, his own family, the priests, his friends, and finally all the people and the king; and besides that, he knew much physical suffering and yet it was Jeremiah who said: "Of this I remind myself, therefore I still have hope: Because of the LORD's mercies we are not consumed; His compassions never fail. They are new every morning; great is Thy faithfulness. The LORD is my portion, says my soul, therefore do I hope in Him. The LORD is good to those who wait for Him, to the soul that seeks Him. It is good if one hopes and quietly waits for the salvation of the LORD."

Lamentations 3:21-26 (Berkeley)

11
Paris in the Springtime

"O to be in England in the merry month of May," or Paris, and why not Rockford, Illinois? A friend of mine was showing some of us her slides from a trip in Europe. After she had flashed on and off the screen a number of beautiful pictures, she came to one lovelier than all the others, so it seemed. Several in the group exclaimed how they wished they too could travel, get out in the world, and see some of the wonders.

Our hostess allowed us several minutes for "exclaiming." Then she told us that *that* picture we were rhapsodizing about she had taken before she left for Europe. It was the sunken gardens across from the Sinnissippi Park in Rockford, a few blocks from where I grew up.

The "lesson" learned that day has helped to keep me mindful to be on the lookout for beauty wherever I am. In the Springtime it is easy to find poetic scenes. You rarely have to look far. Springtime is wonderful *everywhere*.

In Paris (where I wrote this column) the spring specialty are the chestnut trees. They line many of the broad sidewalks on both sides, and spread a sea of green over the Champs Elysées. Springtime is always special. It has a way of suggesting happiness, that things will be better, that there is hope. The trees with their ornaments, the flowers, seem to say, "Look at us! We were dead, but we have come alive!" Yes, there is an aliveness about Spring that stirs all of us.

An elderly, dignified gentleman told me as we walked toward the Louvre, "If I make it to May, I'm always good for another year."

The Springtime holds out her lovely, strong arms and beckons us to come and dance. Even the young and healthy can seem worn by the end of winter, but Spring puts a bounce in their step, as if everyone were wearing new tennis shoes.

Yet, regrettably, the Springtime does not restore everyone. Those with heavy sorrows, and the millions of emotionally and mentally crippled persons around the world, need more than the Springtime to get them going again.

There are so many escapes for those who cannot, or will not face life. One escape is travel. Traveling is wonderful if you are not running away from yourself, but I am speaking about those who travel and see nothing. Some of the "poorest" people in Paris are seated at the sidewalk cafes in front of fasionable hotels and shops. They have wealth, power, possessions, and time, but they are poor, because their souls are empty.

The Lord Jesus Christ said to all men, "I am the way, and the truth, and the life." Here is reality. Here is life. All of the world, the beauty of Paris in the Springtime, you, I, and those at the sidewalk cafes—all will pass from the earthly scene one day, but God will remain. How wonderful to have a faith to live by, and a faith to die by, that will take a person into God's eternity, the true and everlasting Springtime.

John 14:6

A Time to Ponder: It is important to take time to consider who Jesus really is. Read prayerfully John Chapter 14 and Philippians 2:5-11. To think that one day every knee shall bow at the name of Jesus.

12
Watch That Turtle

The prolific writer, Somerset Maugham, in a little book called *The Summing Up*, was telling about one of his grandfathers, a dignified, ugly little man with mischief in his eyes. An old solicitor, whom Somerset Maugham had known when he was a boy, told him about a dinner party he had once attended at the grandfather's house in Kensington Gore overlooking the park.

The grandfather carved the beef, and then a servant handed him a dish of potatoes baked in their skins. As the writer said, "There are few things better to eat than a potato in its skin, with plenty of butter, pepper, and salt, but apparently my grandfather did not think so. He rose in his chair at the head of the table and took the potatoes out of the dish one by one and threw one at each picture on the walls. Then without a word he sat down again and went on with his dinner."

Somerset Maugham asked his friend, "What effect did this behaviour have on the rest of the company?"

The solicitor said that no one took any notice.

Seeing what good it does me to read about other people and their imperfections, I make no apology for sharing a few of my own, hoping someone will be benefitted, even if it is only to say, "Thank the Lord I am not as peculiar as she is!"

I saw a cartoon the other day which spoke to my condition. A wife was in bed with a cranky expression on her face, while her husband was pulling out the drawer from an enormous row of filing cabinets which filled one wall of the room. She said to him, "Do you have to verify *everything* I say?"

I identify with both characters,—the cranky look on the wife's face, for one thing, and then the plodding determination of the husband checking to see if the latest piece of information he has received has any truth.

For example, recently I learned two fascinating things:—One, It is dangerous to kiss a turtle, because they can give you a disease. The author said that it is caused by a bacteria called salmonella. I have never seen a turtle in the mountains of Switzerland, so I cannot verify the statement in the direct way, but who wants to kiss a turtle? And furthermore, my dictionary goes no farther than "salmon."

I wrote that for a column last year. Now I have several new dictionaries which include salmonella, and also thanks to helpful readers, I now have a small file on turtles *and* salmonella. But the second unverified piece of information intrigues me even more.

Last Spring some friends and I were driving in the lovely farmland around Parma, Italy, the home of Toscanini, Parma hams, and Parmesan cheese. The artist in our group asked if we could stop so she could take a picture of the red poppies in a green field, with an Italian blue sky as a background. That led to a discussion about poppies. Do they grow wild in the fields? What happens to the hay? Signora explained in a matter-of-fact way, "The farmers plant the poppies in their fields because it helps to calm the cows."

You must realize that in our car (and often around our table) there are several languages being spoken, and so when Signora's statement was finally translated into English, I was glad I had a tight grip on the steering wheel. I exclaimed, "HELPS TO CALM THE COWS!!" My journalistic mind immediately began thinking about cheese, milk, yogurt. Are poppies the explanation why a cup of warm milk taken at night helps to put you to sleep?...

I was cranky by the time we arrived in Florence, mostly upset with myself for not knowing Italian, so I could go ask a few farmers if it's true that their cows are more calm than Illinois or Wisconsin cows where I do not recall seeing red poppies in the fields.

I consoled myself with the realization that it would take me years to learn Italian, French, and German well enough to run around and ask all the questions that crowd my brain, and I might get so sidetracked on turtles, cows, and poppies that I would not accomplish what I am supposed to with my life. Thousands of people right now are using the glorious gift of life in trivial pursuits. Obviously I am not speaking against the need for recreation, vacations, and good times, but how easy it is to fill one's entire life with that which is vanity, empty, futile.

We are given such a high calling in Christ to lay up for ourselves treasures in heaven, and this is certainly not only for ministers, missionaries, Sunday School teachers, or those more obviously engaged in Christian work; but it is for every born-again believer. My treasures will not be your treasures, because people are different, and God will work through us according to these differences.

Whenever you feel as if what you are doing for the Lord is insignificant, remember with what delight Jesus called to the attention of his disciples the poor widow who put into the treasure chest two mites. He said, "I assure you that this poor widow has put in more than all those contributing into the treasury."

Mark 12:43 (Berkeley)

A Time to Ponder: Our lives involve time, and then the next important ingredient is, how we use the time God has given us. It has been rightly said: "So teach us to number our days, that we may apply our hearts unto wisdom."

Psalm 90:12

13
"It's Your Fault."

The other day, on an inner page of a Swiss newspaper, I read about a bridge that fell into the Rhone River. I would never have noticed the small item, excepting that I had begun to think of that bridge as my bridge. I'll try to explain it.

Simply because you live in a foreign country, you never get over being what you are. I am very American, and so, of course, dependent on a car for every errand. The only way I can fool myself into taking time for a hike is to have a goal in mind. So every evening this summer when I was down in the valley working on a book, at the calming time of day just before twilight, when the trucks have stopped rattling, motor bikes are silent, and little giant-voiced children have been called inside for supper, I would cross a few fields, walk through an orchard, go along a stream tumbling down from the Alps, until I arrived at the Rhone River. And there was my bridge.

On the last inspection I thought to myself, it looks about finished. A little leveling off on the approach on the right bank, a touch here, a touch there, and never again will we have to cross the shaky, one-lane bridge when we go to France.

And so you can see why I kept reading over and over about the bridge that had fallen down. I wanted to be sure it was my bridge. That is what is maddening about a foreign language. When you really want to know something, it becomes excessively foreign. But there it was in plain French. The bridge had fallen down. According to the paper, the loss was considerable, but, no one had been injured. It had fallen down at night.

I took my walk earlier the following day, and even returned at twilight to see how it looked from the other side of the river. It was true, the bridge had collapsed, but having an imagination like one of my small nephews, I have to confess that I was a little disappointed not to have found more of the bridge in the river.

Before going to bed that night, I struggled through the newspaper article once more and began to grapple with the "deeper" meanings. Obviously, if a big bridge falls down, someone made a mistake. But how curious? Almost immediately, the architect announced over TV that it was not his fault. The contractor told a reporter, "I'm not responsible." When interviewed, the engineer and crew let it be known that they were not to blame.

Finally, all fingers began to point to the manufacturer of the metal used in the spans of the bridge. The specialists investigating the accident said that "it appeared as if" the metal had buckled, but at the moment there was no published statement as to exactly what did happen. However, the manufacturer let it be known that he could not in any way be held responsible, because apparently there was an "inherent defect" in the material when it was brought to his factory.

As a friend who also read the article said, "This is a situation which could go all the way back to Adam!" And let none of us forget that Adam said to God, "The woman whom You gave to be with me, she gave me of the tree, and I did eat." And finally we come to the end of the line (actually, it is the beginning) with Eve's response, "The serpent beguiled me, and I did eat."

And doesn't it sound familiar? Is it not the story of your life and mine more often than we care to admit, busily running around either excusing ourselves or accusing others, and sometimes doing both at the same time.

For example, yesterday I dropped a plate, and as it smashed on the brick floor, immediately, I said to myself, "It must have had a crack in it." That was some comfort as I stooped to pick up the broken pieces, but what wiped my slate clean was the added realization that I was not to blame at all. It was the fault of my friend for carelessly putting the plate on the edge of the counter.

What else can we say, what else can we do when we get glimpses of how foolish and funny we are, except to laugh, and then it never hurts to pray:

Dear Lord God, We do believe that You see all, and even know the secrets lodged in the depths of our hearts (as well as those we read about in newspapers), help us to admit before You our faults, our deceptive ways, and our weaknesses. Give us a fresh awareness of Yourself, so that we might see how needy we really are. May we never treat sin as a little thing, nor be so fully employed pointing our fingers at others "worse than we are" that we allow wrong things to go on in our lives that need to be confessed and cleansed by the shed blood of the Lamb of God. Give us the grace and the courage to admit that we are wrong once in awhile.

Then after we are convicted, show us again Your gentleness, Your kindness, and amazing love. We pray in the name of the Lord Jesus Christ, who has given us this day to rejoice and be glad in, and may we ponder anew how wonderful is the mercy and forgiveness of God. Amen.

Genesis 3:12, 13

A Time to Ponder: Sing all the verses of "Wonderful Words of Life," or any other of the beloved hymns which used to be sung at Sunday night church services. Find a church that does meet on Sunday nights. Let's encourage ourselves in our LORD.

14
Do Something!

If you think your home is disorderly, you will derive a sense of relief to hear about the home life of the composer, Alexander Borodin. The apartment at the Academy where Borodin taught was rent-free, but there its advantages ended. His friend, Rimsky-Korsakov, said that the apartment was like a corridor, and there was no way for Borodin to lock himself in or pretend he was not at home.

Students, friends, relatives swarmed through the "apartment" at all hours, especially the relatives. They came often and in large numbers, occasionally selecting Borodin's home as a "convenient hospice to fall ill or lose their minds." The apartment was usually a litter of disorder and disarray, and to add to the chaos, Borodin seemed never to remember whether or not he had eaten, and so meals were fantastically irregular.

And, oh yes, the Borodins had cats, not one cat, not two cats, but lots of cats. Even though Professor Borodin lived in the midst of this carnival with an outward calm, never seeming to mind the invasions of his privacy, he did come down with a succession of headaches, colds, stomach disorders, toothaches, and boils. But as we say, no one is perfect, nor does anyone live in ideal surroundings.

Do you have a song, a poem, a suitcase full of notes under the bed, or an unfinished afghan, a yearning to paint, or some furniture which needs refinishing? Get to work. Your conditions could not be worse than Borodin's!

Alexander Borodin was actually a professor of chemistry, and he divided his busy life among research, teaching, and composing. He thought of himself as a Sunday composer, because he worked at his art only in odd hours. He wrote to a friend once, "I can only compose when I am too unwell to give my lectures, so my musician friends, reversing the usual custom, never say to me, 'I hope you are well,' but instead tell me, 'I do hope you are ill!' "

His great opera, *Prince Igor*, was unfinished at his death. He had worked on it for seventeen years. The 20th century composer, Kabalesky, considers Alexander Borodin one of Russia's greatest masters.

A Time to Ponder: I correspond with a lovely lady who, because of something she read in *Your Life Is Worth Living*, decided to do something different. I'll let her tell you about it. She wrote, "Did I ever mention how the chapter 'Never Die of Ordinariness' spoke to me? Anyway, my life has been rather blah, to put it mildly, for some time, and I have decided to change several things and stop dying of ordinariness. One of the major changes will be that I am starting college this month."

She went on to explain that she had been out of high

school for forty years, and that she never had any intention of going to college then, but now that they were living near a college, she began to get the urge to go. "I go in fear and trembling," she said, "but I am claiming Isaiah 50 verse 7 for the days ahead... One thing I will need special help from the Lord is in the matter of my memory. I have been atrocious lately."

And so now several months have gone by, and yesterday I had another letter. She said, "I thought I would 'report' on how I am making out. I am glad to say that the Lord has done 'exceeding abundant' in helping me." She not only got A in two of her courses, but the psychology course was a real victory. She said, "It was awful. I would read the book and understand what I was reading, and then when I closed the book— nothing. I just could not remember. I told you that my memory was terrible. So I just went to the Lord and told him that he would have to help me remember what I had studied or I might just as well quit. I felt an assurance that He would help me." And so when she took the dreaded psychology test, she not only got an A, but 100 per cent, the highest in the class! "Believe me," she said, "I am not bragging, but giving all the credit to the Lord." She added one other little note, "My husband is inclined to brag on me for the marks I have gotten, but I keep telling him that it is all the Lord and He gets the glory."

"The Lord God is my helper; therefore I am not confounded, for I set my face like a flint; I know that I shall not be put to shame." "It shall come to pass that before they call I will answer, and while they are yet speaking I will hear."

Isaiah 50:7 and 65:24 (Berkeley)

15
What A Difference

Every once in awhile I am like Slorky, the Sloth, out of sorts, spleenful, low spirited. I hate the feeling, and reading *Thus Spake Zarathustra* by the German philosopher, Nietzsche, and listening to record upon record by Delius did nothing to help get the world right side up. But now that the musician has given her lecture on Frederick Delius, the chalet is again filled with cheerful, noble music, and Nietzsche is back on a bottom shelf. I appreciate the point Jane was stressing: "It *does* make a difference in your life what you listen to, what you read, and who you follow."

Nietzsche rejected Christianity and poured his "theories" about life into a number of books which have greatly influenced the thinkers of last century right up to today. No wonder our world is upside down when so many of the leading philosophers, poets, teachers, artists, writers, and musicians follow the teaching of a man who was insane the last ten or twelve years of his life.

If we want to be encouraged, the best place to turn is the Bible. As we claim for ourselves some of God's wonderful promises, we gradually learn that these "bad" days in which we are living can be the best of days for God's faithful children. Many people have confused values today, because we are exposed to so much untruth. The only way back to truth is to read in faith the Word of God, and go where there are Christian people. We Christians are not meant to stand alone.

Many people are in serious trouble today, because they have come to a false conclusion that God's written revelation to us is not reliable. But, the basic problem modern man faces is that of believing in God or not believing. It is no different than the choice Abraham had to make. He "staggered not at the promise of God through unbelief, but was strong in faith, giving glory to God; and being fully persuaded that, what He had promised, He was able to perform."

A Russian Christian philosopher has pointed out, that man's problem and his predicament arise from the fact that he has not only lost the way, but he has lost the address. But it is still not a "new" thing to wonder if there is a caring God. I am reminded of the tenor aria in Mendelssohn's great oratorio, *Elijah*—the haunting beauty of the words, "Oh, that I knew where I might find Him, that I might even come before His presence."

A newsman was watching a missionary bathe a person with leprosy in India. He said, "I wouldn't do that if they paid me a million dollars." The quiet, dignified reply was, "I wouldn't either, Sir."

There are those in the community where I live who agonize and struggle all hours of the day and night with those who have lost the way, listening, talking, opening up the Scriptures, more talking, more listening, and praying—then get up the next morning and fix

breakfast for the ones who have kept them up most of
the night. And believe me, there is more to it than
listening, talking, and cooking, but these friends of
mine at L'Abri and Bellevue would not do what they
are doing for a million dollars either.

They are part of a little company of true believers
around the world working at tasks many people would
think beneath them, but they serve God out of love and
gratitude for what He has done in their lives. Many of
them also have experienced the emptiness and loneli-

ness of living without purpose or direction, and the folly of trying to buy satisfaction and peace.

Both Nietzche and Delius never found joy nor peace in their lives. They had their moments of glory in this world, of course, but as they grew older, everything soured, and as I said, Nietzsche lost his reason.

"It *does* make a difference in your life what you listen to, what you read, and who you follow." And it can change your life if you put your complete trust in the right Person.

Romans 4:20, 21

A Time to Ponder: An air-force captain in World War II was flying near the northern coast of Italy. Because of some mechanical failure, his plane kept losing altitude. When he realized that he was going to crash, he jumped. And he said, "When I hit the water, that's when I began praying. I didn't know I was praying. I hadn't spoken to God since I was a boy, but I kept saying, 'God, if you help me out of this one, I'll be on your side for the rest of my life.' "

The first miracle,—he did not drown, in spite of the fact he became all entangled in the parachute. And the second,—some Italian farm ladies who were working in a field saw him splash into the Mediterranean, and ran to help him when he dragged himself up on the shore.

Immediately they took charge. They got across to him that he was in danger and hid him away from the German soldiers, who also witnessed the accident. These good-hearted women saw that he had enough to eat and drink, and one day indicated to him that it was safe to come out of hiding. The soldiers had gone.

Sometimes it proves to be the best thing that ever happens to us to get pushed down so deep we have to cry out to the Lord. "Then you will call and the LORD

shall answer; you will cry and He shall say, Here am I."
"Without faith it is impossible to please Him: for he
that cometh to God must believe that He is, and that He
is a rewarder of them that diligently seek Him."

Isaiah 58:9
Hebrews 11:6

16
The Loving Thing

The poet, Robert Burns, died at the age of 37, but in his short life he left a legacy of verse in praise of love. Not only love between a man and a woman, parents and children, friend for friend, but love by man to mankind. His life was stamped by poverty and cold January winds, which give his poetry an authority it might not have had if he had lived in ease and comfort. The friends of Robert Burns saw to it that his wife and their four children did not suffer want.

Two of his most familiar poems are "Comin' Thro' the Rye" and "Auld Lang Syne." He was the son of a tenant farmer and did not have the "advantages" of a formal education. Most of his learning came from reading. He studied the best of the English poets. He had a hard life, and as it has been said before, no one is perfect, he had a tendency toward drinking which combined with a long-standing heart ailment caused him to fail rapidly and not live to be forty.

His poems are filled with homely wisdom. In the verse, "To A Louse," he wrote:

> "The social, friendly, honest
> man, whate'er he be,
> 'Tis he fulfills great nature's
> plan,
> And none but he."

> "O wad some power the giftie
> gie us
> To see ourselves as others see
> us."

I am impressed with God's interest in the "little" people of the world. Those who quietly, day after day, live thoughtful, kind, considerate lives. Rarely do you see their faces on television, or their names in the newspapers, but they are very much there. This is one reason that my faith in Christianity is stronger today than it was twenty years ago, from the love I have seen exhibited in the lives of Christians in many places in the world.

Another individual known for his kindness once said, "Years ago it was made clear to me that when I was in doubt as to God's highest will in any situation, if I would do the most loving thing possible, I would always be doing His will." It is always an encouragement to see love in action.

To express love sometimes can be a little bewildering, as in the following situation. Some cousins came to stay for several weeks in my sister's home. Her nine-year-old son, Soren, was thrilled to have boys coming, and one of them his own age. He and Jimmy had a marvelous time, but the last week of the visit they began to be too "friendly" and fought like cats and dogs. One or the other was always crying.

Finally the departure morning came and Jimmy and his brother had to go home. Soren didn't even want to come down and say goodbye. He was crying so hard. He didn't want Jimmy to go. He kept sobbing, "I love him. I love him. I wish he was my brother." My sister said to Soren, "You certainly have a funny way of showing love." He answered, "I love Kathy (his sister), and we fight." At the close of the letter my sister simply said, "I guess I'll never understand children!"

But that is not the end of the story. A letter came the following day from my sister. She said, "The school nurse called me about 10:30 yesterday. Soren was crying. He missed Jimmy that much. I had to bring him home. He cried most of the day, didn't even look at TV. But he is fine this morning. Last night before he went to bed he wrote Jimmy a letter and told him that he really missed him."

As Robert Burns said, "Don't forget the old acquaintances. Bring them to mind." Those of us who live in a far-off land know how healing and cheering letters are.

A Time to Ponder: "Love your neighbor as yourself," was not an accidental lapse of speech. That is exactly what we Christians are supposed to do. As my nephew Soren illustrated, love involves some small disagreements along the way. We do not always agree with ourselves, so we can not expect love to be perfectly smooth. To love, seeing ourselves "as others see us," should make us willing to make allowances for one another. The main thing is to genuinely care, as Soren does about Jimmy. It is a wonderful experience to have a close friend. "The soul of Jonathan was knit with the soul of David, and Jonathan loved him as his own soul."

It takes time to have friends, and even more time to be a friend, but do you think it goes un-noticed by God and His angels when you bake a cake in the midst of a frantic morning and run across the street to the elderly neighbor with a broken hip who lives alone, and bring it, and a word of cheer? Do you think God is indifferent to the faithful wife and mother who takes it seriously that her home shall be a place of stability, love, and joy? Do you think that the LORD who is on the side of the widows and orphans does not see when you visit the lonely and sick in nursing homes, or bring a child into your home who needs caring?

Was it said for nothing, "Though the LORD be high, yet he has respect unto the lowly: but the proud he knoweth afar off." May we be among those who genuinely care for others, and not only pray, but really *do* something to help where there is a need. It will be worth it all one day to hear the King say, "I assure you, so far as you did it to one of the least of these brothers of Mine, you did it to Me."

Matthew 19:19
I Samuel 18:1
Psalm 138:6
Matthew 25:40

(We had another "Titus" letter from our friend, Anne, today. She wrote, "I sold 7 pot holders to the members of the Wed. Bible class Wed, and 5 pot holders, 2 dish cloths to the Volunteers at the Blind center. I earned 12 dollars. Too goodie!! I must make more pot holders and dish cloths. That keeps me too busy and too happy!")

17
Two Small Incidents

Little things, small happenings can have big and long-lasting consequences for good or evil. Did you know, for example, that the infamous feud between the Hatfields and the McCoys started over a hog that both familes claimed to own? How much better for them and their descendants if they had divided the poor pig turning the misunderstanding into a celebration or a picnic!

Instead, they allowed the quarrel to build up, like a windstorm sweeping down a mountain into a valley where nothing can stop the wild wind until it is spent. The bitterness, anger, and hatred between the Hatfields and the McCoys became a way of life for them for more than forty years, and it was not over until there were freshly dug graves on both sides of the fence.

In contrast to the malice and ugliness that resulted from that one small incident, a good deed was done in the late 15th century. It was not a big thing, but a necessary link in the events which finally led to the Reformation.

Everyone has heard about Martin Luther, but if you are like me, I easily forget details. I had forgotten how poor the parents of Luther were until I read a new book on the Reformation. His father worked in a mine, and his mother often had a difficult time caring for the family. More than once she had to go into the forest and gather wood before she could cook a meal.

They were poor people, but not ignorant nor lazy. They reverenced the Living God and served Him as well as they knew how. Martin Luther, no doubt, owed his courageous spirit, sense of humor, respect for work, and his nobility of character to his parents and grandparents. They imparted to him something else which is priceless to have in any century in which one lives:— common sense.

The parents were eager for their bright son to have an education, and before he was five, Luther was sent off to school. Because of his fragile health, his father or a friend often had to carry him to town. As he grew and learned, he was later enrolled in a school sixty miles from home; but there in Magdeburg he became ill and was forced to return home after one year.

When he grew stronger, Luther was sent to Eisenach, which is near the famous Wartburg castle, where later he translated the New Testament into German. There was a good school in the town, and this plus the fact that Luther had relatives there gave his parents the hope that they would help him.

But they did not, or could not, and Martin Luther, along with other poor students, was forced to go into the streets and sing for his daily food. As he was not a healthy person, the strenuous, uncertain life affected both his body and mind. Not only his health suffered, but so did his studies, and he became discouraged.

It was then that the "little thing" took place. A certain Mrs. Ursula Cotta, a kindhearted, sensitive lady, asked the young Luther if he would like to live with them. She greatly enjoyed his singing, and after the "serenades" she had become aware of his thoughtfulness, thankfulness, and quickness of mind. And his need.

The husband of Ursula Cotta was a wealthy merchant, and in their comfortable home Martin Luther not only received love and nourishing food, but for the first time in his young life he came under the influence of the Renaissance, which stimulated his eager mind and gave him a thirst for a wider culture and knowledge.

Living in the Cotta home helped to refine the manners of Luther, but happily not too much, or he would not have been the prickly, outspoken individual God needed as his voice in that decadent, agitated moment in history... These were happy, good years for Luther, and he was able to finish his high-school studies with honors which opened the door to the university and further study. One other benefit he received in the culturally-rich home of Conrad and Ursula Cotta was their love and appreciation of music. They encouraged him to sing and play the lute, which became a vital part in keeping Luther, under all his stresses, the balanced, wholesome person that he was.

When I think of the positive things which are ours because of the reformation,—freedom, to mention only one of the great results, it makes me thankful that Martin Luther found friends in Eisenach. God's man for that needy time in history, after such a long period of religious turmoil, unrest, and great dissatisfaction all over Europe, needed all the training and education and wisdom possible to take his stand for truth. He shook the world when he began preaching Bible truths.

When I consider Thy heavens, The work of Thy fingers, the moon and the stars ... What is man, that Thou art mindful of him? Psalm 8: 3, 4

Little things, small happenings can have big consequences for good or evil. Few of us have the gifts of Martin Luther, and the world is over-populated with the foolish, arrogant Hatfields and McCoys, but how much better your town and mine would be if more of us had the spirit of Ursula and Conrad Cotta.

A Time to Ponder: "Blameless in the day of our LORD Jesus Christ." Dear God, May we think about it again, how amazing, how liberating to know that people like you and me, with faults and blemishes (some days leaning on all sides), are considered even today blameless in God's sight, because of what Christ has done for us. Help us to serve you with joy and shine as beacons in this crooked and perverse world. Amen. Read Philippians, Chapter two....

I Corinthians 1:8

18
No Short Cuts

"I have been trying all my life to like Scotchmen," wrote the great essayist, Charles Lamb, "and am obliged to desist from the experiment in despair." He says very honestly, that he is a bundle of prejudices. Some night when we are counting our blessings, we should total our prejudices too. It is always healthy to get things out in the open; then, by the grace of God, we can do something about them.

But with all his prejudice against the hardy folk from Scotland, I believe that even Charles Lamb would have appreciated Andrew Bonar, this firm, but pleasant man of God, who devoted his life to telling others about his Lord and Saviour.

Andrew Bonar, the great writer and minister from Scotland, was known for his firm belief in the profound truths of Scripture. Because there was no wavering in his faith, God gave him a joyous and triumphant hope about life which he was able to communicate to thousands of others. He was known to be a man of deep and fervent prayer. He did not believe in short-cuts to Christian living. In reading through his Diary one is amazed at the frequent references to prayer. "Christ and Him crucified" were at the center of his thinking, preaching, and living.

He went to bed one night not knowing that this was his moment to walk through the valley of the shadow of death. True, he was past eighty, but still very willing to go on if the Lord would have him. But living or dying, Andrew Bonar was the Lord's, and those in his family who were at his bedside that night saw him go through a very restless time, and then, suddenly, the struggle was over. He grew quiet. A look of profound peace came on his face, said one of his relatives, an expression of delight and surprise, as if he had suddenly and unexpectedly found himself in the presence of his beloved Lord and Saviour with whom he had walked over sixty years here on earth. And do not let the news-media fool you into believing that the 19th century was any easier to live in than the 20th.

Last night I was reading about Madame Guyon, a great lady of faith, who suffered deeply for our Lord in a black and bleak moment in history, the age of Louis the Fourteenth (one century before Andrew Bonar). It took many years of struggle and unhappiness, before her eyes were opened to the great Scriptural doctrine, "the just shall live by faith."

This changed her life, as it did Martin Luther's, John Wesley's, and all of us born-again Christians. But before it happened to her, she marveled when two of her friends who met for the first time and seemed immediately to understand each other. She said in awe, "They conversed together in a spiritual language."

One of the joys for me in being a small part of the L'Abri Ensemble which has toured in the United States and Europe once or twice a year for over ten years, relates to what we are speaking about. Every place we go we meet people we have never met before, and yet it is as if we have known each other all our lives, and we speak together in the language of Christian love and thankfulness.

A Time to Ponder: May this be a day of rejoicing for all of us as we think about what is implied in the statement: "The just shall live by faith." Two things come to my mind right now: Because of our faith in Christ, we are safe now from whatever it is that would alarm us, besides the wonder of being saved forever. As the psalmist sang: "Lift up your heads, O ye gates; and be ye lifted up, ye everlasting doors; and the King of glory shall come in." "Now unto him that is able to keep you from falling, and to present you faultless before the presence of his glory with exceeding joy, to the only wise God our Saviour, be glory and majesty, dominion and power, both now and ever." ....

Psalm 24:7
Jude 24, 25

19
Oranges and Theology

One of my favorite little people is Jeremy Kidron Popp. He is a young man now, but some things you never forget. It is related to a saying of O. Henry:

"You can't appreciate home 'til you've left it, money 'til it's spent, your wife 'til she's joined a woman's club, nor Old Glory 'til you see it hanging on a broomstick on the shanty of a consul in a foreign town."

And you cannot fully appreciate people until you have almost lost them... When Jeremy was four-years-old he wandered away from home. In exploring the world beyond his yard, he came upon a house under construction. Being a curious lad, he pulled at a plank that was sticking out in an inviting manner. It unbalanced a bricklayer's scaffold and about 300 pounds of brick, dirt, and boards fell on Jeremy.

His mother estimated that he must have been buried for fifteen to twenty minutes, his feet doubled under him and his head and arms pulled back. Later he told her, "I tried and tried to lift it, but it was too heavy, and

86

I called you, and I called Daddy and Timmy, and I called Jesus too. I prayed to Him," and he added sadly, "but I couldn't fold my hands!"

Jeremy was rescued by a neighbor who had stepped to his back door to check the lock before going to work. The neighbor said that he had no idea why he opened the door and stepped out on the porch for a minute. But the important thing was that he did. It was then that he heard a feeble cry from beneath the pile of debris.

Jeremy walked "crooked" for several weeks, but there was no permanent damage to his spine. I saw him shortly after the accident. He came running toward me in a funny, sideward way and jumped into my arms. With his usual, shy grin he said, "I was almost killed dead."

While his mother was talking on the telephone he took charge of entertaining me. First he ran to the kitchen and came back with an orange for me. He disappeared again, and soon returned with two more oranges for himself. He made an attempt to peel one, but gave up, and so I had three oranges. In order to absorb some of the juice (I hate peeling oranges), I put a newspaper in my lap. This proved to be a conversational piece. Suddenly Jeremy said, "There's one God..." Then he thought a moment as he popped a slice of orange in his mouth, and frowned as people do who are about to make an original statement. "No," he said, "there's two gods—Jesus and the Devil. Jesus reads the Bible, and the Devil reads the newspaper."

After this burst of knowledge, he ran to the kitchen for more oranges. I confess that it is the same with me. When I talk theology, I get hungry. At this point, Jeremy's mother joined us. While he was in the kitchen getting her an orange, I shared what her son had just told me. When he returned, together we tried to make it clear to him that the newspaper is not exclusively Satan's territory, that many fine and good people not only read newspapers, but have some part in putting them together.

Jeremy was unimpressed. He simply repeated his thesis and went for more oranges. The deeper we dipped into the theory that the Devil reads the newspaper, the more it began to make sense. The Devil not only must read newspapers, but he must read them with relish, and he must read the front pages with the satisfaction of an author seeing "his work" in print. War, crime, famine, rape, robbery, etc....

Many theologians today think that it is not "20th century" to believe in a real Devil, but they are wrong. Paul had a word about those who twist the truth and make it less than what the Scripture says: "God never sent these men at all; they are 'phonies' who have fooled you into thinking that they are Christ's apostles. Yet I am not surprised! Satan can change himself into an angel of light, so it is no wonder his servants can do it too, and seem like godly ministers." He added these stern words: "In the end they will get every bit of punishment their wicked deeds deserve."

It is impressive how much even a child can learn from godly parents. Jeremy was troubled that he did not fold his hands when he prayed for help, but he knew enough to call to the right Person in his trouble, and God heard his prayer and sent the neighbor to rescue him.

II Corinthians 11:13-15 (Living Bible)

A Time to Ponder: Only the naive, foolish, and ignorant among us dismiss Satan and say he is not at work. We see too much on all sides that shows he is very active. But we need not fear. There is a place of safety.

"And it shall come to pass, that whosoever shall call on the name of the Lord shall be saved." God's great promise of salvation includes lots of "lesser savings" along the way, as well as the final great moment when all those who believe in the Saviour will begin their heavenly citizenship.

Acts 2:21

20
"Where Did We Go Wrong?"

In one of the popular women's magazines recently, there was an article written by a mother of a 16-year-old daughter. The mother described herself, her husband, and the family as church-going, middle-class people who live in an attractive home in a good neighborhood. Overnight their comfortable lives were turned into a nightmare. They accidentally discovered that their young daughter and her friends had already experienced and tasted acts of immorality and depravity, which the mother associated only with the worst element of society, never with young people from "good" homes. When the daughter was confronted with the evidence, the parents expected the girl to crumble before them "in shame and guilt."

The mother said, "But her reaction was the worst horror of all. She was affronted to think she was going to be cut off from her best friends. She did not see anything wrong with the lives they were living."

Repeatedly the mother asks the question, "Where did we go wrong?" And there are thousands of other bewildered parents around the world asking the same question. Toward the close of the article the mother gave a possible clue to where she is wrong. She said, "I cannot reconcile myself to what has happened to us and to our child. I refuse to accept responsibility for it. Society must bear the burden—our affluent society with its emphasis on materialism, its de-emphasis of spiritual values, its glorification of the banal and the mediocre."

As a friend of mine often says, "When you are pointing your finger at someone or something else, do not forget, there are three fingers pointing back at you." There will be no healing of any of the ugly wounds in our lives nor in the lives of others until we, as individuals, accept some of the responsibility of where we are today.

It won't do to shift the blame to society. Who is society? Unfortunately, *we* are society—the bewildered parents, the defiant daughter, her friends, and you and me. Society is like an orchestra. It's no better than the poorest player. Each instrument is important if there is going to be a pleasing sound.

And what about our affluent society? It is as Goethe once said, "Everything in the world can be endured, except continual prosperity." Then why don't we (at least those of us who call ourselves Christians) return to a more simple life? It was not said for nothing that life is more than nourishment, and the body more than clothes. Christianity is more readily caught than taught. It would not hurt those of us hungering for better lives to review the life of our Lord. Never can we imitate Him perfectly, but there should be some motion in that direction.

The entire article, "Where did we go wrong?" made me think of what the great scholar of the 5th century, Jerome, said. "I shudder when I think of the calamities of our time. Indeed, the Roman world is falling; yet we still hold up our heads instead of bowing them... Who could believe that Rome has fallen, who could imagine that the proud city, with its careless security and its boundless wealth, is brought so low that her children are outcasts and beggars?"

Who could believe that Rome could fall? Who could believe it? I can tell you that there are many of us living in the last part of the 20th century who can believe it, because we are seeing "signs" ourselves; and unless there is a real turning back to God and the true and good values in life, we could yet experience these sobering words, spoken by that most human of the prophets, Jeremiah: "O Lord, the Hope of Israel, all who forsake Thee shall be put to shame; those who turn aside from Thee shall be written on the ground,* because they have forsaken the Lord, the fountain of living waters." *(From which their names will soon be obliterated.)

There is a prayer written by King David, about 1500 years before Jerome, and nearly 3,000 years before the close of the 20th century, and it is still fresh, good news to all who pray it in faith: "Have mercy upon me, O God, according to Thy lovingkindness: according to the greatness of Thy compassion blot out my transgressions."

"It is with men as with wheat," said a man by the name of Cooke. "The light heads are erect even in the presence of Omnipotence, but the full heads bow in reverence before Him."

Jeremiah 17:13
Psalm 51:1

A Time to Ponder: One of the marvels in living is that each one of us who has our brief moment in history is given the possibility of choice. We either choose to believe the Living God and follow the written revelation He has given to us about Himself in the Bible; or we do not believe God and go our own way. And we have overwhelming evidence today that going one's own way is devastating.

Take time (or make time) sometime today and read carefully Psalm, Chapter 51, Isaiah, Chapter 53, and John, Chapter 1. It is so encouraging to fill one's mind with the Word of God, and also to read about those who have had faith in the past, and how God helped them.

Last week I was reading about William the Silent, the Prince of Orange. The story of his life and the terrible struggles of the Dutch people to be free and able to worship God according to the Scriptures is one of the great episodes in the drama of the reformation. All those who love freedom should respect William the Silent. His rise above accumulated losses, dire humiliations, and amid ever-bursting disasters can only be explained by his faith in God.

It is as the Lord Jesus Christ has said, we are to enter through the narrow gate. The way that leads to destruction is broad, and as we look inward and around, read our newspapers, books, and magazines and watch TV, it is plain to see that many are on it.

How do you enter the narrow gate, someone may ask? By recognizing, thanking and praising the God of all history who sent His Son to die for us.

I saw a picture in a Christian magazine last week of an old man, a leper, who lives in Korea. He has nothing that you and I might count as important, but I wish you could have seen the smile on his face. He, like the Prince of Orange, and many of you who read this page, has made his peace with God. Wars, rumors of wars, illness, crime, corruption, cheap living, hunger, nothing can take away the hope and joy which Christ puts into the hearts of His people.

"Enter ye in at the strait gate: for wide is the gate, and broad is the way, that leadeth to destruction, and many there be which go in thereat."

"In all thy ways acknowledge Him, and He shall direct thy paths."

Matthew 7:13
Proverbs 3:6

21
Whom Shall I Fear?

The Swiss bridge that fell into the Rhone River a few months ago is still sagging, but there is hope that it is going to stand again. Leaning over it, like a prehistoric bird or an anxious mother, stands a tall crane. A workman puttering at something at the foot of one of the pillars saw me looking at the fallen bridge. Obviously he was glad for a spectator and dangerously lurched out over the river holding on to a rope with one hand and swinging a pail in the other. He grinned at me when he was safely back on land and said something in Italian.

"So they're going to prop up the bridge?" I said pointing to the crane and lifting my hands. Obviously we couldn't have much of a conversation, but something sounding like "imbeciles" and "idiots" frequently came into his speech. It was clear that he thought it a poor plan to try and patch the bridge, that it would be better to start over. By gesturing I let him know that I had no intention of driving over that bridge. He laughed, waved his arms, twisted his head (who can out-gesture an Italian?) and let me know that *he* wasn't going on the bridge either!

But having said that,—once the bridge is properly repaired, undoubtedly we both will drive over it many times. Anxiously the first time, perhaps, and then we will forget about it. There is a time to forget in life, and particularly about little matters. Don't let small things build up. The Italian workman and I both know that the Swiss are careful, deliberate people. This was a rare happening—a bridge falling down in Switzerland. It was kept rather quiet.

On the day it is announced that the bridge is ready to be used, I promise you it will be a solid, unshakable structure which probably shall outlast you and me by a few hundred years. We will be able to drive on the bridge with no anxiety.

Two friends were talking the other day about the inconsistency of fears. Your fears are not my fears, nor mine yours. I heard someone say yesterday, "I wouldn't get on a plane if you gave me all the gold in France." Whereas, many of us love to fly and think nothing of it, except that we enjoy it.

One of the young pastors in our community prayed recently that we would remember to be kind to each other, because some in our midst are shy and fearful of other people. It is easy to have fears, and it is curious how a small matter of anxiety can cripple our minds and bodies almost as effectively as something big or deep-rooted.

Then think of all the unnamed fears we have, and the ones that are foolish. I know you will laugh at me, but a tiny mouse gnawing in the thick beams which make up the outer walls of our old chalet can keep me awake for hours at night. I keep trying to develop the carefree spirit of Beatrix Potter and Walt Disney who found mice such adorable creatures, but have not succeeded yet. No one's perfect.

I think it helps to remember that fearfulness is not normal. It is related to our fallen condition. Have you ever had the experience of praying just before going to bed for some loved one in trouble, and then instead of leaving the person and his problem with the Lord, you spend half of the night wondering and worrying? That is when it is good to recall the words of a favorite hymn. "Like a River Glorious, is God's Perfect Peace," by Frances Ridley Havergal is a good one to have tucked away in the mind for an occasional sleepless night.

It is true that when we become Christians we leave behind many of our fears, but surely not all of them. I think fear is like growing older. It will be "around" all the days of our earthly lives, but,—and this is an important but,—it need not rule our lives, nor ruin them. If I were asked to describe in a few, simple words my idea of heaven, I believe I would say it is a place where there is no fear.

Do you remember when homes used to have Bible verses hanging upon the walls? Here are a few, not only for your kitchen and bedroom, but to be etched upon our hearts to remind us where to turn when fear-ful:

"What time I am afraid, I will trust in Thee."

"The Lord is my light and my salvation: whom shall I fear? The Lord is the strength of my life; of whom shall I be afraid?"

"We may boldly say, The Lord is my helper, and I will not fear what man shall do unto me."

Psalm 56:3
Psalm 27:1
Hebrews 13:6

97

A Time to Ponder: The gifted English poet and musician, Frances Ridley Havergal, who wrote many beautiful hymns, was for a number of years a very unhappy, fearful Christian. She was a mixture of reserve, sensitivity, and gay bursts of buoyant temperament, and even her sisters did not know of her inner conflicts and times of real agony. She wrote in later years, "Many have thought mine a comparatively thornless path, but often, when the path was the smoothest, there were hidden thorns within...."

She was a dedicated scholar, loved nature (was "ecstatic" over her first glimpse of the Alps), and her thirst for knowledge was lifelong. One time while studying her Bible she came upon these verses: "O wretched man that I am! who shall deliver me from the body of this death?" Then she turned to First John, in the first chapter and read these words: "If we say that we have fellowship with him, and walk in darkness, we lie, and do not the truth: But if we walk in the light, as he is in the light, we have fellowship one with another, and the blood of Jesus Christ his Son cleanseth us from all sin."

Suddenly, the Holy Spirit gave her insight. She was reading the New Testament in Greek (she was fluent in seven languages), and she saw for the first time that the word "cleanseth" is present tense; and so it really means, the blood of Jesus is ever-cleansing us.

It was a revelation to her, and from that time on she no longer grieved over her sins nor allowed fear to have dominion over her. She quietly accepted the truth that "if we confess our sins, he is faithful and just to forgive us our sins, and to cleanse us from all unrighteousness."

In spite of frequent illnesses and a brief life (she died at 43), she had much mirth and joy in her Christian living. She shared this joy with many others, and through her penetrating writing in such hymns as

"Take my Life and Let it Be," and "I Gave My Life for Thee," she has reached and moved a multitude of souls all over the world.

I John 1:6, 7, 9

"Like a river glorious is God's perfect peace,
Over all victorious in its bright increase;
Perfect, yet it floweth fuller ev'ry day,
Perfect, yet it groweth deeper all the way.

"Stayed upon Jehovah, hearts are fully blest,
Finding as he promised, perfect peace and rest."

22
The Same Old Question

Around the holiday season nearly every family with small children goes through it again,—the question, is Santa Claus real? The following incident took place in the home of friends: One night at dinner, in the midst of a conversation which had nothing to do with Christmas, a six-year-old boy asked, "Is Santa Claus really real?" His parents gave him a few answers in the manner of the famous editorial, "Yes, Virginia, there is a Santa Claus," which appeared in the *New York Sun* about seventy years ago, and some of the guests around the table presented their theories all favoring a real Saint Nicholas. One uncle even added a few "ho,ho,hos."

The boy listened thoughtfully to each explanation, but you could tell by the way he was biting his lower lip that none of the answers were convincing.

"Well," he said finally, piercing clean through the shallow arguments with one well-aimed arrow, "if Santa Claus is real, how come he don't die?"

The mother corrected his English, and in the brief silence which followed one could hear Walter Cronkite giving statistics about how much money merchants were losing over the holidays due to shoplifting (someone had forgotten to turn off the TV set in the living room).

"You see, Gary," the boy's father said at last, "well, it's this way, I mean ... uhummm, it's difficult to explain," he added lamely, and began again, "Well, you see, Santa Claus is sort of a tradition, yes, that's it, he's a tradition."

The boy winced at the word, tradition, obviously having no idea what it meant; but he came to his own wonderful understanding, and in the midst of another adult conversation which had started up, he said loudly,

"Well, then, I'm going to take some of that tradition myself, so I won't die either!"

And either a little before, or after, Walter Cronkite from the living room gave his parting message, "And that's the way it is."

Quickly I must add, I am not speaking against the lovely world of fantasy. I believe strongly in make-believe and am thankful for authors who took the time and effort to write such books as *The Wind in the Willows, Charlotte's Web, The Tale of Mrs. Tiggy-Winkle, Alice's Adventures in Wonderland, The Book of Nonsense,* and *The Adventures of Nils.* And how drab would life be if there were not people like Ray Valine, a garbageman in Sacramento, California, who the week before Easter dressed up as a rabbit and passed out candy from an Easter basket to hundreds of children along his route. For the Fourth of July he wore a top hat and distributed balloons to the excited, waiting youngsters. And, of course, at Christmas he was a jolly Santa Claus, presents and all.

This is the right way of make-believe. The children knew all the time that the colorful character who jumped down from the garbage truck was that nice man, Ray, who liked playing games with them. Please, lawmakers, do not do away with Santa Claus and Easter bunnies. We need them as much as we need home-made apple pie or a concert in the park on a hot summer night.

What is needed is to put things into proper categories. If children have the capacity to understand and get excited about Santa Claus at an early age, they can be told the story of the Lord Jesus Christ, but with one difference. Santa is make-believe, Jesus is not.

Why deny children the wonder of the fact that all who believe in Christ have the seed of everlasting life in them now? Charles Wesley, one hundred years after Mendelssohn wrote the joyful, triumphant music to "Hark, the Herald Angels Sing!"—gave us these beautiful and true words:

> "Hail, the heaven-born Prince of Peace
> Hail, the Sun of Righteousness!
> Light and life to all He brings,
> Risen with healing in His wings.
> Mild He lays His glory by,
> Born that man no more may die,
> Born to raise the sons of earth,
> Born to give them second birth.
>
> Hark, the herald angels sing,
> 'Glory to the new-born King.' "

Born that man no more may die. But someone will, ask or should ask, "How will the dead be brought back to life again?" We all know people die. Any time I want to I can picture in my mind the tombstones that border the express highway which leads from the International Airport into New York City. There must be several cemeteries, because on both sides of the busy highway, as far as you can look, are rows and rows and rows of graves, markers, monuments and a million dusty artificial flowers stuck in the ground. This is death at its ugliest. Do not think I am trying to talk about death in a cheap, easy way, but to ignore the subject is even worse.

One of my nieces told me that she and her five-year-old daughter have spoken together about death several times. The child keeps bringing up the subject. (I have been told that this is not unusual in alert children.) She said that after they had had one of their little talks together, she got the idea (from reading First Corinthians Chapter 15 in the *Living Bible*) to buy some seeds, several different kinds, and the two of them planted the seeds.

Then on the days and weeks which followed, whenever they'd remember in the midst of much busyness, they watched to see what had happened. It was impressive, she said, to see the differences in each plant. Then gently one day my niece spoke about the fact that it was the same with our bodies. They will die, be put into the ground like the seeds, but one day they will rise again, and God says that our old bodies will be glorious new bodies.

Again I say, I am not pretending that it is simple to speak of death, nor is it easy to write about. We live in a scarred world since the fall of Adam and Eve. There is something in our flesh that does not want to think about dying, let alone speak about it; but when others ask us, we should have something to say to them that is not make-believe. If we are Christians we should know our Bibles well enough to turn to the passages which bring comfort, not only because of the beauty of the words, but because they are true.

A Time to Ponder: It is worthwhile to read all of First Corinthians, Chapter 15, and in two or three versions to get the full force of the words. For our consideration at this moment I will quote I Corinthians 15:35-37, 42, 43:

> "But someone may ask, 'How will the dead be brought back to life again? What kind of bodies will they have?' What a foolish question! You will find the answer in your own garden! When you put a seed into the ground it doesn't grow into a plant unless it 'dies' first. And when the green shoot comes up out of the seed, it is very different from the seed you first planted... In the same way, our earthly bodies which die and decay are different from the bodies we shall have when we come back to life again, for they will never die. The bodies we have now ... become sick and die; but they will be full of glory when we come back to life again. Yes, they are weak, dying bodies now, but when we live again they will be full of strength."

23
Foretelling the Storm

God's gifted people are generally ahead of their time. Albrecht Dürer whose dates are 1471 to 1528 seems chronologically far from the last quarter of the 20th century. But we can learn more from his paintings and drawings than from many of the "artists" exhibiting in our art galleries and museums today, who are completely out of touch with reality and truth.

Dürer was a painter, an engraver, and a maker of woodcuts, and he is generally acknowledged as the greatest of all German painters. Even today he is considered to be one of the greatest painters of all time. His technical gifts were staggering, and his engravings and woodcuts alone would have been enough to establish him as a master.

The intellectual power and the moral force of Dürer are as great as his technical genius. He had the Renaissance man's passionate curiosity to learn the secrets of the world, but not in an arrogant spirit. He did not reject God's world as so many of the 20th century exhibitors have done, but he investigated it with profound interest in the framework of the Scriptures. Because Dürer worked within the Reformation structure, he had the freedom to deal with universal subjects without throwing away the detail and significance of even a small piece of sod which he painted, or the beautiful watercolor of a columbine he did two years before his death. His drawings and paintings of the animal world are well-known and beloved.

Albrecht Dürer was born in Nuremberg, Germany in an age of tremendous intellectual and spiritual upheaval, and he learned the goldsmith trade from his father. The history of his forefathers, like that of Bach, leads us back to Hungary. One could do an entire study on Bach and Dürer, and it would be impossible to do it without including Martin Luther. These three mighty men have much in common, and overshadowing them all is not only the spirit of Christianity, but the reality of the Christian faith.

Dürer did not have a happy marriage, and there were no children, but he found his consolation in God and in his art. His trips to Venice and all he saw and learned in Italy were central to his whole work.

Dürer did a great trio of engravings called, "Melancholia." They are really a prophecy of modern man. Then there is his work entitled, "St. Jerome in his study," which is a complete contrast to the engravings about dissatisfaction and melancholy. It shows the love of reading and studying. Everything about it breathes peace. The true peace that is based on content; as it says in Numbers: "Hath He said, and shall He not do it? or hath He spoken, and shall He not make it good?"

One of the first masterpieces of Dürer was the series of sixteen woodcuts he made of "Revelation"—The "Apocalypse." The book of "The Revelation" has repeatedly attracted the attention of mankind, particularly during stressful times in history. Because there is much interest in the future today, these woodcuts are very timely. Dürer completed the series in the same year as Leonardo da Vinci was doing his fresco, "The Last Supper," in Milan, Italy, and at the same time Savonarola was being killed in Florence for his religious stand.

Dürer's "Apocalypse" was not a commissioned work. He printed it himself in both German and Latin. He made it overlarge in size to impress the importance of it, also so that people who could not read could be given the Word of God. It was a real picture book, but not like Salvador Dali's "Revelation" which is a dream world. Dürer's woodcuts represented reality as it should be, future, past, and present. A critic once said, "The sensitive nerves of art can always foretell the storm before it breaks." But even better and more certain than the nerves of the artist is the believing in what God has revealed to man, and sharing the truth with others.

As one studies these works, one is deeply impressed with the technique of the artist,—his strength, the firm lines, amazingly intricate detail, the beauty, and the truth of what he is presenting. We have the right to be indignant and angry at much of what we see exhibited in galleries today. There is lack of content, lack of technique, lack of energy, and most surely lack of inspiration.

Numbers 23:19

A Time to Ponder: It *does* make a difference what you believe in life. It is not only essential for a theologian to have the right doctrine, and then live it, but also the artist, the housewife, the politician, the schoolteacher, the author, and the roofer. It is exciting to study the

24
"Snow, Beautiful Snow"

On a visit in New York city a few years ago, I stopped to have a cup of coffee in a small restaurant off Fifth Avenue. I sat at the counter, and while I was waiting to be served, the lady to my right began talking to me. She had received part of her order, and was trying to get the attention of the waitress for the rest of it. In front of her was a sweetroll, but no knife to cut it, nor butter to put on it. The pot of tea was there (and had been for ten minutes), but no cup nor saucer. It wasn't that the waitress was busy, but her attitude brought forth sparks all around the counter. It was a struggle the whole way. We never did get spoons.

I learned that my new acquaintance was a nurse from Great Britain. "I'll be so glad to leave New York," she said, stirring her tea with her knife. "In England you rarely find such poor manners, but I am sure things are not as bad in other parts of the States."

I assured her that if she really wanted to find friendly

people she should visit Rockford, Illinois. She went on to tell me that she was taking care of an elderly lady who lived in a beautiful apartment on Park Avenue. She said that her 90-year-old patient had everything that wealth and position can secure for a person. Her health was good, considering her age, but she was miserable, and doted on making everyone else miserable. "She's one of the most difficult people I have ever cared for," said the nurse. "She's stingy, mean, and has the same manners as our little waitress. She is not one bit grateful for the privilege of a long life, but just mad that she is so near the end and will have to leave all the so-called 'good things' behind."

What a contrast she is to my friend, Elizabeth, who for many years helped to keep things lively at the River Bluff Nursing Home in Rockford. She lived to be 102. I enjoyed her, because she was full of fun. She was always telling humorous stories, mostly about herself. She told me once that she didn't think too much about the old people in the home who sat around and did nothing. "They think I'm a clown," she laughed. Then she exclaimed seriously, "I'd rather be a clown than a vegetable."

I do not have to tell you that the following poem was not written by the 90-year-old lady who lives on Park Avenue, nor the waitress in the coffee shop. No. This little poem came from the heart of one who was at peace with God, and looked out on His world with appreciation, and thankfulness. The room where she lived was very small, and she shared it with another lady who was blind. She told me once confidentially, "I wouldn't have taken this bed by the window if my friend had her sight, but she can't see, so the window is mine." She took a long look out of her window. In all simplicity she said, "That window means more to me than I can ever put into words." Then she added impatiently, "Some of these *old* people here don't even notice when the seasons change!" Elizabeth did:

"Snow, beautiful snow
That covers the ground all white
If it didn't come every winter
Our fruit and vegetables would blight.
Because it sends down moisture
Down deep where rain often washes away.
So come every winter,
But don't stay *too* long,
Because our seeds must be planted in May.

> I made this up—ha, ha,
> Elizabeth"

A Time to Ponder: The great American dramatist, Eugene O'Neill, whose father was a popular actor and his mother, eventually a morphine addict, was raised in cheap hotels, and though he lived to be a successful writer, he was never happy. He did, at one time, live in a beautiful home, but around 1950, when he had given up hope of ever writing again, he and his wife moved into a Boston residential hotel. O'Neill never left the hotel except to visit doctors. One day he said, "I knew it, I knew it. Born in a blank blank hotel room and dying in a hotel room."

The famous composer, Beethoven, who also lived a tormented life in rebellion against the Living God, died shaking his fist at his Creator.

Dear Lord, we know that You want to save people, but we know You will not be mocked. Our part is to believe and trust You. We thank You for the promise that You guard the footsteps of Your worshipers. May we indeed worship You in words and deeds, In our Saviour's name, we pray. Amen.

111

George Whitefield wrote in his diary: "Did anyone yet ever trust in the Lord and be forsaken?"

"I shall be satisfied, when I awake, with Thy likeness..." "The LORD is a God of judgment: blessed are all they that wait for Him." "He is faithful that promised."

Psalm 17:15
Isaiah 30:18
Hebrews 10:23

25
Learned to Fly

Once or twice a year I disappear from Huemoz, closet myself in a hotel room to recover, rest, think, and eventually, to write. In a moment of weakness (on one of my writing trips), I gave the telephone number of the place where I was staying to the ardent gardener, who is also the director of the Golden Egg Inn.

Whenever I talk into a public telephone in a small hotel, I feel as if the waitress who serves my meals, the maid who cleans the room, the young boy who vacuums the hall, and certainly the manager who plugs me in, are all listening. Thus I limit my conversation to a series of mumbled "yes's," "no's," and "hmmmmmmmmmmm." However, it is more difficult to control the people with whom you are speaking.

Loudly she said,

"You haven't asked about the chickens?"

When I said nothing, as I was occupied—trying to get into the right position to prevent a cracked eardrum (I hate telephones), *she* continued,

"Just because you're off there writing a book doesn't mean you can forget your family!"

I groaned,

"Hmmmmmmmmmmm."

"What did you say? We seem to have a bad connection. Aren't you interested in the chickens?"

I tried to make my "yes" sound bright.

"Well," she said cheerfully, as one settling back to recite a favorite poem, "Esther, per usual, was standing in the middle of the food pan when I brought out the leftover spaghetti. Edith, white and prim, was on an upper shelf making low, disturbed sounds. She doesn't like her sisters. Mary was singing, and Winifred's learned to fly."

"FLY!!!" I bellowed into the phone, completely forgetting myself. Immediately I lowered to "Hmmmmmmmmmmmmm."

"And Josephine and Roberta..."

"Can't you talk about anything else?" I whispered desperately. "What will people think?"

"What do you mean, what will people think?" she demanded. "Are you in a broadcasting studio or on TV or..."

I hissed lowly,

"It's the manager and the maid."

"Are they in the phone booth with you?"

"No, of course not, but..."

She sniffed,

"It is about as satisfactory talking to you on the telephone as it must have been with Calvin Coolidge!"

"Hmmmmmmmmmmm," I replied firmly.

"There is definitely something wrong with our connection," she complained. "Every once in awhile I hear a strange humming sound. Could you please repeat what you said. No, skip it, as our time is running out, and I have one more important thing to tell you. Herr

I hate Telephones !

Lengacher has gone for the wood, and..."

"For the bookcase?" I said with enthusiasm.

"No, of course not, for the new chicken house. Don't you remember? We drove the stakes in the ground before you left."

And so the conversation naturally returned to the hens and their exploits. Every once in awhile I managed to get in "Hmmmmmmmmmm."

Finally she said,

"The humming sound is getting so bad, I'll have to hang up. I'll write and tell you the rest. Goodbye. Hope you're getting on with your writing."

"Thanks for calling. Bye Bye!!" I sang out cheerfully and loudly.

A Time to Ponder: I believe the book I was working on at that time was "Away With Complaining," and as the ardent gardener enjoys telling our guests, "She's been complaining ever since!" This sort of humor which involves teasing, kidding, exaggerating, whatever you want to call it, is very American. It has been interesting to me to notice how humor differs from country to country.

I remember once being on a ship going to Turkey, and there wasn't a person I could talk to, because of the language barrier. Suddenly from an upper deck I heard several people laughing. Something about the spontaneity, the wholesomeness of the sound convinced me they were Americans, and it didn't take me long to get up there and get acquainted and join in the innocent fun. All people laugh, of course, but few laugh as freely and openly as we Americans do.

"A merry heart doeth good like a medicine: but a broken spirit drieth the bones."

"To everything there is a season, and a time to every purpose under the heaven." Personally, I am thankful there is a "time to laugh."

Proverbs 17:22
Ecclesiastes 3:1, 4

26
In Search of
an Apricot Tree

In Solzhenitsyn's first novel, "One Day in the Life of Ivan Denisovich," there is a crisp, shattering picture of what happened to millions of Russian people in the years 1922 to 1953 under Joseph Stalin. He writes about Ivan, a political prisoner in one of the many Siberian labor camps, who is helping to build a wall in weather that is more than 20 degrees below zero. The foreman has given orders to hurry up the job, and to dump the excess mortar over the wall to save time. It doesn't matter to him how poorly the work is done. All he is interested in is getting it done.

He shouts again at Ivan, as it grows darker and colder, "Let's be off," and he seizes a hod and climbs down the ladder. But not Ivan. The Russian author said, "The guards could have put the dogs on him now, it would have made no difference." He ran back to look around. Not bad, he thought. He ran over and looked along the wall,—to the left, to the right. Good and straight. His eye was true. His hands were still good. Then he ran down the ladder.

It is a theme in the writing of Alexander Solzhenitsyn: Do the *right* thing no matter where you are, what your circumstances, or if everyone around you is cheating, lying, and stealing. You do not have to imitate wrong doing. The admonition: "Let your light so shine before men, that they may see your good works, and glorify your Father which is in heaven," is not only for Sundays or among our Christian friends, but in our place of work, or while shopping, or traveling, and yes, in prison. In some places it seems almost impossible to stand against the crowd, but it is astonishing how a little light in a dark place glows. Even after eight years in the brutalizing atmosphere of a Communist labor camp, Ivan had not allowed the generally accepted corruption to change his standards. It was only a crudely-made wall far off in Siberia, but he took pride in his part of the job. He was the sort of man who hated waste, and worried about every little detail of work.

Solzhenitsyn was born in 1918, the son of an office worker and a schoolteacher. He graduated from a university with a degree in mathematics, and at the same time took a correspondence course in literature. In 1945, while he was a captain in the Russian army, he was arrested for making some comments about Stalin in a private letter to a friend. For this he spent the next eight years in labor camps, and another three in exile. In 1953 when Stalin died, he was released. Before he began teaching in a secondary school, Solzhenitsyn spent some months in a hospital being treated for cancer.

His books, like most of the Russian classics, are difficult to start and it is easy to mix up the characters, but once you get into one of his books, you will never regret making the effort.

There are episodes in the *Cancer Ward* and *The First Circle* which are unforgettable and have enabled me to be more thankful for freedom, and a lot of "little" things which are so easy to take for granted.

His writings reflect a knowledge of the Bible, and there is the feeling of Christian truth behind many pages. An intellectual in an earlier century once wrote:

"When I survey the occurrences of my life, and call into account the finger of God, I can perceive nothing but mercies. Those who speak of crosses, afflictions, judgments, misfortunes ... to me have proved to be in the end favors of a heavenly Father."

There is a spirit in *Cancer Ward*. When I finally put down the book, I was both crying and laughing. The main character, Oleg, had gone to the hospital expecting to die, and the day he is dismissed from the cancer ward, you too enter into his joy at being alive. It was the morning of creation for Oleg. Everything was new to him and had to be understood afresh. It was Springtime, and God was renewing the face of the earth.

> "For winter's rains and ruins are over,
> And all the season of snows and sins ...
> And frosts are slain and flowers begotten,
> And in green underwood and cover
> Blossom by Blossom the spring begins."
>
> *Swinburne*

Oleg had one desire before he had to take the train and go back into exile. He wanted to see an apricot tree in bloom. The description of his search for a flowering apricot tree is tender and moving. It left this reader humbled and awed at the nobility and beauty God gives to those who stand for freedom and truth in the midst of our corrupt and evil world.

Dear Lord, Forgive our lack of dedication and our

dulled senses of appreciation and thankfulness. Help us even this day to lift our eyes upon the tiny corner of the world where You have put us as if we too have been in prison, in exile, in a cancer ward, and are stepping out this moment into the first day of a new life. Give us the feeling of early-morning springtime joy as we renew our Christian vows. Help us by Your grace to begin to live as God's children ought to live, delighting in You, Your creation, and the varied, curious, and challenging people all around us who need to know God's love through our caring. Thank You, and we pray in Jesus' Name. Amen.

Matthew 5:16

A Time to Ponder: Thomas Wolfe, the gigantic young man who wrote and did everything gigantically (this included his faults, his deficiencies, his weaknesses), picked up one day a line from an old *Punch* parody, "I'm sure there is Something, Somewhere if we could only find it," and from this "text" he wrote the novel, "You Can't Go Home Again." And that is the way he lived and died, homeless and always hurrying away from some evil he could not define to some ultimate good he could never attain... Is there some one you know who needs Jesus? If He is your Friend, share Him.

27
Making
the Most of Life

Not long ago I received a letter from a student in Texas who is a junior in college. She wrote,

> "Dear Miss Carlson (or anyone else in the L'Abri Fellowship), I'm not really sure how to begin this letter, as I've never written one like it before. I wish there was someone like you or Mrs. Schaeffer that I could talk with to find the right direction for my life.
>
> "I realize, however, that no person can give me peace. I know I must settle my questions and doubts with God,—but I don't know how. My desire is to have the most exciting life imaginable. I don't want to miss anything."

("Bravo," I shouted, which had an unsettling effect upon our cat, Mother Owl, resting in my reading chair. I couldn't help it. I love enthusiasm. I read on with interest)—

"Part of me believes that God will give us that kind of life," she said, "and the other part pulls the other way. I don't want my Christian life to be ordinary. Most of the Christians I know live relatively dull and sheltered lives." Then she added honestly, "As a matter of fact, so do I, and I'm tired of it. I really want to know what life is all about, and I want to make the most of it."

She said more, but we have enough to think about. How would you answer such a letter?

I say it solemnly, first I prayed. It is great gain to know how limited we are humanly speaking. I could be no help to her if I leaned to my own understanding. On my desk I have a prayer. I do not know who wrote it, but over and over it speaks to my condition. It is called "Prayer Answered." In thinking of my new friend, I also thought of my own life:

> "I asked for all things that I might enjoy life: I was given life that I might enjoy all things. I received nothing that I asked for, all that I hoped for, My prayer was answered."

In that vein, in the spirit of contradiction which is a part of Christian truth, I attempted an answer. First I told her that I was mailing a few books which try to show that the Christian life is anything but dull. Then by airmail I sent the "Twenty-five Basic Bible Studies" by Francis Schaeffer (when there is a spiritual battle being waged for a precious soul, it is no time to economize). I explained that these studies would help her with her three basic questions: One,—To find the right direction in life. Two,—How to settle the questions and doubts about God. Three,—How to have a life that really counts.

Gently I tried to say that in the midst of her enthusi-

astic desire to have "the most exciting life imagina-
ble," she must not be foolishly romantic about the
Christian life, and settle for something less than true
Christianity, which will be only an emotional experience and soon peter out.

Those of us who have lived through those early
"high-spirited" days know to the depths of our hearts
that life is like a patchwork quilt. It is a colorful mixture of hard knocks, joy, sadnesses, dancing on clouds,
work, and more work, fun, boredom, and losses almost
too much to bear. We live to see our high spirits sink to
low, sometimes, very low. A friend who has been in a
down-under experience tried to describe it: "I feel
rather like a deep sea diver," she wrote, "after a pro-
longed time in very deep water who needs time before
she's been able to re-enter a 'normal' atmosphere.
Meanwhile she has explored the depths of some interesting new territory, found exciting treasures, new
fears, special deliverances and has come up gasping,
but a richer woman!"

Her vivid picture reminds me of Hebrews 12:11,
concerning the disciplining that all believers go
through from time to time. We do not enjoy the "low-
spirited" days. "Chastening," in the words of Phillips,
"is in fact most unpleasant."

But always in life, for the child of God, comes the
"nevertheless afterwards" time. Again in Phillips'
translation: "Yet when it is all over we can see that it
has quietly produced the fruit of real goodness in the
characters of those who have accepted it in the right
spirit."

In the letter to my friend who does not want to live a
dull and sheltered life, I slipped in one paragraph urging her not to look for perfection in other people, particularly Christians. Some,—not all, but some of the
seemingly "dull and sheltered" Christians who go in

and out of church faithfully, and have worn, used looks, are God's people who *have* grappled with the sorry evidences of sin, decay, and imperfection in our fallen world, and they are weary and discouraged. Prayer, encouragement, and a sense that others care for them is what most people need,—not criticism. Criticism when we are already down is bad medicine, and for some, even a small dose may be fatal.

Let us thank the Lord, that at any hour of any day, we may pray as David did when he was ashamed of himself for living so far beneath what God has in mind for His people: "Thou knowest my blundering; my guilt is evident to Thee. May those who have their hope in Thee not be put to shame because of me ... O God, I am afflicted and in pain, let Thy salvation set me on high ..." Then David, as if he is speaking directly to you and me, added: "You who seek God, let your heart revive! For the Lord hears the needy."

Hebrews 12:11 (Phillips)
Psalm 69:5, 6, 32, 33 (Berkeley)

A Time to Ponder: Toward the end of the letter that I wrote to the enthusiastic one who wants to make the most of her life that it is all gain to be a Christian. If she commits her life to Christ now, and by the help of the Spirit begins to live a praising, thankful life to God, she not only will have exciting times, but a lot more. God never works the same way in lives. He respects the individual.

Perhaps there is someone reading these words who has never put his foot down and said, "Lord, I want to follow You too." The Giver of good gifts always responds with kindness and authority: "Obey My voice, He says, and I will be your God, and you shall be My people; walk in all the way that I shall command you, that it may be well with you."

According to the first letter to Timothy, God's purpose in the world is that all men should be saved and come to realize the truth. That man of enthusiasm, Paul, put it this way: "This statement is completely reliable and should be universally accepted:—Christ Jesus entered the world to rescue sinners."

> "I asked for power that I might have the praise of men;
> I was given weakness that I might feel the need of God.
> I received nothing that I asked for, all that I hoped for,
> My prayer was answered."

"So to the king of all the ages, the immortal, invisible, and only God, be honor and glory for ever and ever."

May all be well with you too.

Jeremiah 7:23 (Berkeley)
I Timothy 2:4, 1:15, 17 (Phillips)

125

28
An Independent Spirit

In our rush to understand the culture of the later part of the 20th century we sometimes tend to forget the flow of history and certain bright spots which enrich us, rather than distress us as so many things do today. I would like to call to your attention the composer, Franz Joseph Haydn. His music has cheer, beauty, logic, order, and a freshness of imagination at a moment in history when most of these words are foreign to our whole "modern" climate.

Haydn respected God and the order in His creation. He did not run after the revolutionary ideas of Jean Jacques Rousseau, who was recklessly urging the thinkers of the middle of the 18th century to uproot ancient habits, remove laws, and return to the natural conditions as seen in savages and animals. No, Haydn accepted life as it came to him,—hard, at times, and yet there was always the possibility of turning the hard times into something good. His music reflects his wholesome attitude about life. It is clean, sensible, and optimistic. And what interests me,—Haydn wrote some of his finest and happiest music toward the end of his life. He said on one occasion, "God gave me a cheerful heart, so He will surely forgive me if I serve Him cheerfully."

He had a simple background, born in a music-loving peasant family. The parents instilled into their children a love for work, method, cleanliness, and above all, faith in God. As a boy he spent nearly all his time in church or in school. While he was a choir boy in Vienna (and it must be emphasized that Haydn was brimming with humor and pranks), he could not resist cutting off the pigtail of a fellow singer. He was put out of the choir, although there were a few other circumstances which led to his dismissal.

For a period of time the young Haydn had a meager existence giving lessons and playing night serenades in the streets of Vienna, but he had already set his heart and mind on a life of music regardless of difficulties, and with unusual calmness he persevered through several years of poverty.

Again, like Dürer, Haydn had a very unhappy marriage, and one could say that it dragged on most of his life. It is a long story, and the details too complex to discuss at this time. Finally, Haydn was appointed the musical director in the country home of Prince Paul Esterhazy, and here he served nearly thirty years under circumstances which were ideal for his development as a composer. There was always something musical going on, and he had to provide the music. As he explained, "I was cut off from the world; there was no one to confuse or torment me, and I was forced to become original."

Haydn wrote for all kinds of instruments, and he is often referred to as the father of the symphony and the string quartet as we know it today. The quartet was Haydn's natural way of expression,—organized simplicity.

One writer declared that after listening to Haydn, he always felt impelled to do some good work! This observation could not be made about many of the 20th century composers. They more often irritate the listener, occasionally enrage him; but after the first shock of hearing Berio, Stockhausen, or Boulez, I find that I am bored; and never have I felt like doing some good work after listening to Schoenberg, particularly after he introduced to the musical world the twelve tone row.

Haydn met Mozart in 1781. A deep friendship followed and both composers learned from each other. When Haydn was invited to go to London about ten years later, Mozart wrote to him, "Dear Papa, You were never meant for running around the world, and you speak too few languages." Haydn replied, "The language I speak is understood by the whole world." And off to London he went, at the age when many people begin thinking about retiring. In this period Haydn wrote some of the richest and happiest music of his life, but it was a sad time too. He never saw his young friend again. Mozart died at the age of 35 in 1791.

Haydn was not so concerned about making the world better. His hope was to make people happier. The "Surprise" symphony is the best known of the twelve London symphonies. The title comes from the andante movement where there is a surprise chord "to wake up the audience." Haydn said that he hoped it would make all the women scream!

Haydn was never in a hurry. In fact his talent developed slowly. With infinite carefulness he attempted to master the over-powering influence of the past, and dare to express himself—to put into music his true self.

He became one of the most independent spirits in musical history, and one of the most deliberate and disciplined.

Certainly it is true that Bach and Handel had a clearer Christian witness than Joseph Haydn; but nevertheless, one recognizes the Christian base in his work. I am reminded of the words of Christ in a discussion He had with His disciples. He said, "He, who is not against us, is for us."

Mark 9:40

A Time to Ponder: A few years before his death, Haydn wrote to some admirers of his in the German town of Bergen on an island in the North Sea. They had encouraged him at a time when he really needed it. Haydn wrote, "Often when contending with obstacles that interfered with my work, and I felt it a hard matter to persevere, a secret feeling within me whispered: 'There are but few contented and happy men here below; grief and care prevail everywhere; perhaps your labors may one day be the source from which the weary and worn, or the man burdened with affairs, may derive a few moments' rest and refreshment.' What a powerful motive for pressing onward!"

We can be thankful that Haydn pressed on. We have a desperate need for his kind of sanity and joy today. I think I'll go put on the "Chicken" symphony. It is charming, healthy music, better than taking vitamins.

29
A Long, Gray Day

If you had peered down at Huemoz from a higher point last week, you would have seen nothing. Even Marinette, who works in the post office, said that it was one of the thickest fogs she has experienced in the Alps, and it lasted seemingly forever, three or four days.

When we inched our way up to Villars on Saturday morning, the musician and I felt as if we were on a perilous mission, and all we were trying to do was to bring in the groceries for the evening meal. And so Sunday morning when I opened the balcony door and saw that it was more of the same, hastily I shut it and drew the curtains. "What's it like outside?" the singer called from her room. "Nothingness," I reported. She sighed loudly, "It's going to be another long, gray day."

Shortly after breakfast, she disappeared into the fog in the direction of the chapel to practice the organ before the church service began. Wearily I said that I'd be down after I did the dishes. I kept trying to rub the gray off the plates. The fog seemed to have penetrated the kitchen. Already the day seemed so dull, so heavy, so long.

When the dishes were done, I put on my raincoat and started down the path to the chapel. I had gone only a few steps when I heard the telephone ring. Groping my way back, I ran in and answered it. "Yes, yes, yes," I said, and then with mounting excitement (all the gray gone from my voice), "OH YES! Wonderful, good, excellent, of course, with pleasure we'll be looking for you around three! Grand!" And I raced dangerously to the chapel to tell Jane who was coming that very afternoon. The long, gray day suddenly had become too short.

I tried the door, but the substitute organist had the door locked. I tried waving at her through a window, but she was concentrating on the organ keys. Then I tried tapping gently. She had pulled out all the stops. At one point I considered smashing the window, but I realized in time how foolish that would be. It would have to be something more dramatic than that to get her attention. At last I decided to leave her alone, let her practice. After all, she hadn't played the organ in over a year, and under the best of conditions it is poor technique to excite a musician before a performance...

In a quiet moment before the sermon, she turned to me and said, "WHAT were you trying to tell me out there?" "Shhhhh," I said, "I'll tell you later." She hissed, "Tell me NOW." As softly and calmly as I could, I whispered, "The Governor and his wife and two carloads of dignitaries are driving up from Geneva to visit Huemoz this afternoon."

Perhaps you are wondering why I did not mention what governor of what state in what country, but to Jane Stuart Smith, Mary Johnson, and all the children at Bellevue, there is only one state, and that state is Virginia. This enthusiasm for the land which has given us eight presidents and Anne Bates, the former director of the home for children with cerebral palsy, has been going on for many years, and the thought of the Governor of Virginia visiting our tiny community was not one bit real.

How Jane could play the organ so calmly, I don't know; and I was a little fearful she might slip in a measure or two from "Carry Me Back..." to you know where. But she played well, and it was short and rhythmic, and surprisingly, so was the sermon, and soon we were back in the chalet trying to decide what to do first.

Immediately we cancelled all thoughts of Sunday dinner. We did not want to take the time, nor did we think it suitable to have the house smell of Vaudois sausage, leeks, and garlic; so we put on our working clothes and cleaned Chesalet from top to bottom, as well as the chicken house. We had been meaning to do the Spring cleaning for weeks.

While I was polishing the copper in the living room, the Virginian called our Bellevue neighbors to tell them the astonishing news and to prepare for a state visit. It must have been one of the children on the phone, because I heard Jane say, "Well, let's see,—a governor is like being the President of Switzerland or the King of Sweden or..." "OOOOOOO!!" squealed an excited voice on the other end, which wiped out the last trace of fog and gloom in the chalet...

And so the distinguished guests arrived, and after the introductions we all sat around, rather stiffly, in the sparkling Chesalet living room sipping tea, and discussing the fog outside, the fog in Geneva, the fog all around the lake, and the fog coming up the mountain. The room and my spirits began to get gray again, when

GOLDEN
EGG INN

Two Fowl Experts
The Singer and Signora

suddenly, the Governor's wife, who had gone to school
with Jane, asked if she could visit the Golden Egg Inn.
The heaviness lifted, and the fun began.

After the chicken house was inspected by several in
the official party and they had been told that these

remarkable fowl had helped to pay for the organ in the chapel, the dignitaries were shown the asparagus bed, the seeds having come from a garden in Pulaski, Virginia. Soon it was time to visit our friends up the hill, and so we all paraded up the steep path, various guests helping to carry the musical instruments, Bibles, a music stand, and two dozen eggs from the Golden Egg Inn.

As we walked into the dining room where we have the Sunday music hour, the children, the staff, and many friends from L'Abri Fellowship burst into "Dixie." Some of the children were waving Confederate flags and banging drums, triangles, and cymbals. This was followed by the singing of "Carry Me Back to Old Virginie."

There was laughter and joy, followed by a program of guitar music, recorders, vocal numbers, and original poetry. We finished the hour with a medley of hymns in three languages. Then the visiting guests went around and shook hands and spoke personally to the children. Danny, the only American patient, had a friend take a picture of the Governor and himself with his new camera. As Erika, the beautiful girl we call the princess said later, it was one of Bellevue's finest hours.

I did not get to say a proper goodbye to all the visitors, because I got pinned in between two wheel chairs talking to Jean Jacques and Daniel who decided *that afternoon*, that they were going to be governors when they grew up, and they wanted to know how to spell "The Honorable Linwood Holton, Governor of Virginia, Richmond, Virginia," so they could write to him later and ask more about it.

And so it goes in this little, foggy village in the Swiss Alps.

A Time to Ponder: I suppose it still was gray and foggy when we finally returned to our chalet, but we didn't notice it. That visit did so much for all of us, and we prayed that our guests would be rewarded for their kindness in coming up the mountain on that gray Sunday. There is a meditation I would like to share with you. It is from a small devotional book given to me over thirty years ago. In the front I have noted that it was not put into use until ten years after it was presented to me: "However perplexed you may at any hour become about some question of truth, one refuge and resource is always at hand: you can do something for some one besides yourself. When your own burden is heaviest, you can always lighten a little some other burden. At the times when you cannot see God, there is still open to you this sacred possibility, to *show* God; for it is the love and kindness of human hearts through which the divine reality comes home to men, whether they name it or not. Let this thought, then, stay with you: there may be times when you cannot find help, but there is no time when you cannot give help." (George S. Merriam)

30
Strong Language

Have you recently seen a morning break forth young and beautiful? I did yesterday. It was my morning to carry up the garbage before the truck arrived. Up the steep hill I stumped in my bathrobe, bedroom slippers, and raincoat (not that it was raining, but it was the handiest thing to slip on). I was irritated about three points: The Swiss government, the French language, and me. One, The Swiss government for telling property owners that they must put out their garbage cans within two hours before the arrival of the pickup truck. Two, the French language, because it always makes things sound so important (at least to me; some of the neighbors pay little or no attention to these IMPORTANT ANNOUNCEMENTS). Three, Me. Who isn't grumpy doing household chores at 6:30 A.M. on a brisk morning?

But when I started back down the path, I lifted my head and began looking around. There were wild crocus in the field beside our chalet not a bit grumpy as they lifted their heads in the direction of the rising sun. The mountains were still capped in white, and the one we call "Old Handel" had a lacy cloud across his forehead as if he had started the day with a mild headache. The red bush, which we bought thinking it was a dogwood tree, was tastefully framed with the delicate yellow-green of the weeping willow and the brown fence.

If you haven't been in the country recently, go quickly while the forsythia is in bloom, and there are daffodils, red tulips, and wild flowers growing in a pasture with several newborn lambs. But with the high price of gasoline and oil, one thinks twice about driving only for pleasure.

Speaking of oil,—there is so much oil in the canton of Switzerland where we live that they are probably planning to turn the streets of Aigle into canals to help channel the overflow. Then we can glide about in gondolas, as they do in Venice, only we will be swishing through oil—not water. But one thing I know: The price which was doubled awhile back will not come down. And do you know who is partly to blame? You and me. We complain only to each other, and not to the ones who need to be told.

Did you hear about Bruce Helm in Seattle? He became so angry when the legislators in the state of Washington voted themselves a 193 percent salary increase that he began to circulate a petition. He needed 118,000 signatures in three weeks. The people caught on so quickly that 700,000 signed! When the vote came up, 80 percent of the voters rejected the salary hike and it was reduced from 193 percent to 5.5 percent.

A story like that makes me want to cheer. We should cheer. We go around assuming we can do nothing about injustice. We Christians, of all people, should not be silent in the ugly face of evil and unfairness. Every time I read Matthew, Chapter 23, I keep hoping the Lord is going to send somebody else to rebuke those who are binding heavy burdens on the shoulders of other men, but that is not the way of Christianity.

Christ showed us with His own life that *we* are to expose those who are lying and cheating. His denunciation of the Scribes and Pharisees involved strong language.

"Woe to you, Pharisees, and you religious leaders!" He said. "You are like beautiful mausoleums—full of dead men's bones, and of foulness and corruption. You try to look like saintly men, but underneath those pious robes of yours are hearts besmirched with every sort of hypocrisy and sin."

When William Booth was a young pastor, he found it difficult to stay in his church, because he found such needy people in the streets and pubs of London. For this he was criticized and called to appear before a conference of churchmen. At the meeting he explained how he and his wife had been able to help some poor people who were ashamed to go into a church building, and he felt God was leading him into full-time evangelistic work.

He requested that he might be allowed to do this; but to his surprise, he was turned down. After some discussion, a compromise plan was proposed. Everyone at the meeting agreed to this, but not William Booth's wife, Catherine. She jumped to her feet from where she was sitting in the gallery, waved a handkerchief at her husband and sang out clearly, "NEVER!"

People looked with shock at one another in this awkward moment, but William Booth answered with a smile and a wave of his hat, met his wife at the foot of the stairs, and that is how the Salvation Army began.

"No," "never," or "absolutely not" are splendid

words when spoken at the right time, but the difficulty today is that there are so many causes that need righting, it is hard to know which one is worthy a good strong "no," "never," or "absolutely not." If we are in doubt, it is wise to wait upon the Lord for the precise moment. But in the meantime we can always put in practice the other half of God's truth and go and speak a kind word to someone who is weary or wandering.

As the Scriptures tell us:

"Dear Friends, if anyone has slipped away from God and no longer trusts the Lord, and someone helps him understand the Truth again, that person who brings him back to God will have saved a wandering soul from death, bringing about the forgiveness of his many sins."

Matthew 23:27, 28
James 5:19, 20 (Living Bible)

A Time to Ponder: Is there something in your community going on that you know is wrong? Have you ever prayed with some friends that God might show you a solution? Talk is the easiest thing we all overindulge in. As James wrote, "Remember, too, that knowing what is right to do and then not doing it is sin."

Daniel's words are an encouragement: "Those who are wise—the people of God—shall shine as brightly as the sun's brilliance, and those who turn many to righteousness will glitter like stars forever."

"A word fitly spoken and in due season is like apples of gold in a setting of silver."

James 4:17 (Living Bible)
Daniel 12:3 (Living Bible)
Proverbs 25:11 (Amplified Bible)

31
One Day
You Will Understand

Corrie Ten Boom, in one of her books, tells of a time when she and her father, who were in business together, went through difficult days. There were many bills to be paid, and no money; the mother was seriously ill; that, combined with other trials, made it all seem insurmountable to her. One dreary morning, she asked her father, point blank, if he felt there was any hope for them. Very carefully he answered, "My girl, don't forget that however deep we have to go, underneath us are the everlasting arms of God."

Impatiently she brushed off his answer, "How does that help us in this moment?"

"It makes all the difference," the older man said with sureness and dignity. "One day you will understand it."

Many years later when Corrie Ten Boom and her sister were herded into a concentration camp and pushed into a crowded, bleak, stinking room and then shown a filthy mattress upon which they were to sleep, she prayed in quiet desperation to God that He would give her a word of comfort to share with her sister at that dreadful moment. She said, "The Lord brought back to my mind father's words spoken so many years ago, and I whispered to Betsie, 'Underneath us are the everlasting arms.' She didn't respond right away, but I shall never be able to describe for you the peace that came into my heart when she whispered back, 'Yes, and what a security it is—these arms will never, never let us go.' "

A Time to Ponder: That story reminds me of an old Scottish minister whom I knew years ago. He had choice things to say, and with his quaint accent he said them choicely as well. Once after he had a group of us laughing at one of his apt expressions, he said, "It's good to hear ye laugh, but don't forget to hold in mind what I said for the day when you'll need it."

And I should like to remind you and myself to hold in mind, for a day when we might need it, what the father of Corrie Ten Boom said to her, "Don't forget that however deep we have to go, underneath us are the everlasting arms of God."

And sometimes you have to go awfully deep in life.

"The eternal God is thy refuge, and underneath are the everlasting arms: and He shall thrust out the enemy from before thee."

Deuteronomy 33:27

141

32
We're Not Getting Younger

From time to time in our Swiss community we have church suppers. Being in a reckless frame of mind one night, we volunteered to be the hostesses for the February meeting. On several occasions we have had fifty or more guests for a buffet supper, but that has been in the summertime when at least half of the people fill their plates and go out and sit in the garden...

And so arrived the night of our church supper. Fifty-five members were expected. Deep snow outside. Of course, everyone arrived in boots, heavy coats, sweaters, scarfs, blankets, etc. As Chalet Chesalet is more like a summer cottage, there is no vestibule, no row of closets, no hall. Everyone comes stamping and shaking off snow directly into the kitchen. Soon the floor was carpeted with boots. In one corner of the small room our pastor was talking with a member who was going through a difficult time, squeezed on the wooden seat which divides the kitchen and dining room, were two adults, one baby, and three children. We put two strong men in charge of swiftly moving the people out of the kitchen into the dining room, living room and upstairs.

Then at least six or eight others remained in the kitchen to be "helpful." I never felt so squashed in all my life. We finally got the food to the table by skipping, dancing, and falling over boots and helpers. When the final large pan of meat loaf was removed from the oven, the singer of our music box chalet, who also enjoys gourmet cooking, swept a few of us aside to put into the oven her Virginia cheese biscuits. She made several batches, and they disappeared as fast as if they had been gold pieces.

And so the guests ate and ate, talked and laughed, then there was music and a time of prayer, and finally the church meeting began. These meetings fascinate me. *Invariably* someone brings up a ridiculous, tiny, insignificant, non-consequential point, which could have been decided by two elders before the meeting (taking perhaps two and one half minutes, maybe three); but instead it is brought up before the group, and like a magnet, it draws out controversial comments and philosophical observations from all the eloquent ones in our congregation (and we have some eloquent ones). To hear their solemn words you could almost be persuaded that it was some life and death decision being made. The *only* way to stop the flood of words is to jump in with another piece of business.

That very day I had received a letter from a member of our church who, under trying circumstances, was going to have to be fitted for dentures. Not wanting to call attention to the person in need, I told the former opera singer (she has a louder voice than I have and knows how to get people's attention) to say that we knew someone, a respected, beloved person, who had a medical problem and that we felt our church should help her.

Somehow, the way Jane said "medical problem" whetted the appetites of mischievous ones in our group as to what was the nature of her medical problem. Jane hemmed and hawed, so finally, from my corner of the room I said, "It's a dental problem." There was dead silence. One practical church member asked, "Doesn't she or he have any insurance." We replied, "None."

Then a voice lying on the floor was heard to ask, "Could you elaborate on her dental problem?" Jane, the musician, came on with raw emotion, and with fire in her eyes and voice, shouted, "Her teeth are falling out—she needs dentures!"

Showing the perversity of the heart of man, including all our church members, this brought forth a roar of laughter (this was why, in the first place, we did not want to specify the problem—we were afraid they might laugh). Then the singer (who is a bit mischievous herself) shook her finger at the young man reclining on the floor, "I hope I'm around when all your teeth fall out, and we'll see who'll be laughing then!!!"

O, these meetings. It gives me hope that the church triumphant is still marching on. Happily, it does not depend on frail, foolish mankind, but it goes on because of the One in whom we have placed our confidence.

When the laughter subsided, Jane meekly proposed that we send our friend $100. I rose up from my corner as if I were at an auction and said, "Make that 200, or forget it." Immediately it was seconded, everyone voted yes, and that was that.

The girl who helped us put Chesalet in order before the supper had brought her baby with her (we usually have one or two unwed mothers in our community).

144

She was a wonderful help, and around four, after I had made the meat loaf and a few other things, I decided to retire to my room to rest before the festive evening.

Alas, the baby and all that goes with tiny infants was lined up in my study.

At the end of the saga: When Jane went to her room to prepare to go to bed in the early part of the morning, after we had restored some order to the downstairs, she found a wet diaper (from another baby) beside her bed. We began laughing, decided to have a small party, recalling that we hadn't eaten since noon. It was a memorable time of laughing and talking about how much we care for all these wild, wonderful people in our church, and we didn't forget to thank the Lord for giving us lives that are different, but rarely dull.

A Time to Ponder: And if it is not your teeth or hair falling out, it is your ears, eyes, throat, or stomach which no longer seem to function properly; and as if that is not trouble enough, one day it comes upon you that you have "lost your mind,"—like in my case.

Suddenly I find myself like Mr. Jellyby (you recall,—Mrs. Jellyby's husband)—I am on the verge of saying something, even opening my mouth; but I can't remember the name of the person I want to tell about, and when (O happy moment, the missing name comes floating into my cluttered mind), I have forgotten what I was going to say...

Generally, not always, you can tell a person's age by how many pairs of glasses he (or she) owns. I have seven. One pair for driving on sunny days, another, for gloom and shadows, still another for drawing, and then there is that pair I wear for smiling at friends while walking about; naturally, I have reading glasses, and typing glasses; and, of course, I have an emergency pair in case I lose all the others.

This is what is colloquially known as "middle age," a bothersome, boring affliction, particularly if you live in a time (as we do) when the news media treats middle-aged people as if they did not exist, or worse.

Occasionally you read an article or column directed at those of us in our middle years, counselling us to slow down, don't eat so much, put away your dreams and begin to prepare for the "declining" years; or more often you hear,—look young, think young, be young. Both extremes are utter nonsense.

The Scriptures teach a better way of life. Forget your age! It is not the important issue. We all grow older. It is as natural as breathing. You cannot hold it back.

If we are living in God's presence because of our faith in His Son, we can experience the exhilaration of mounting up with wings as eagles—at any age. "A merry heart doeth good like a medicine: but a broken spirit drieth the bones." It is not one's age that makes the difference between a good life and a miserable one. It is the attitude we take in the moment in which we live.

I read about a lady in Tennessee who learned to read at the age of ninety-one. She said that she wanted to learn more about God. The article went on to say that now, after several months, she is able to read the Bible fluently; and she has also learned to write, so she can copy favorite passages from Scripture into her notebook.

Dear Lord, If there is some reason why we have stopped "to live" for a few months or years, revive us and make us conscious of the preciousness of time. Renew us, O God, so we might meet our present circumstances with strength, courage, and faith. Thank You, Heavenly Father, and even this day we will rejoice in what Your hands will accomplish through us. In the name of Jesus we pray. Amen.

Proverbs 17:22

"You are old, Father William,
    the young man said,

147

And your hair has become very white;
    And yet you incessantly stand
on your head—

Do you think, at your age,
    it is right?

In my youth, Father William replied
    to his son,
I feared it might injure the brain;
    But now that I'm perfectly sure I have none,
Why, I do it again and again."

—Lewis Carroll

"All the world's a stage,
And all the men and women merely
    players.
They have their exits and their en-
    trances;
And one man in his time plays many
    parts,
His acts being seven ages. At first the
    infant..." (and on through the ages)——
            "The sixth age
    shifts
Into the lean and slipper'd pantaloon,
With spectacles on nose and pouch on
    side;
His youthful hose, well saved, a world
    too wide
For his shrunk shrank; and his big
    manly voice,
Turning again toward childish treble,
    pipes
And whistles in his sound. Last scene of
    all,

That ends this strange eventful history,
Is second childishness, and mere obliv-
ion,
Sans teeth, sans eyes, sans taste, sans
everything."
"As You Like It"—Shakespeare

33
The Comfort of Laughter

Here I was writing about the inconvenience of teeth falling out, when in the morning mail I received the following item in a letter from a friendly correspondent—

"Dear Abby: I am employed at a very large convalescent home. One of the elderly residents here lost her dentures, so with a pillow case in hand, she crept into the rooms of the other occupants while they were sleeping, and picked up each pair of false teeth from the water glasses. She then returned to her room and tried each set until she found one that fit her." (She returned the other dentures, as the letter reported, but regrettably not quite in the same order). The employee continued: "The next morning, everyone was walking around the place with overbites and underslung jaws, complaining bitterly that their dentures didn't fit! How do we straighten out this mess?"

—Denture Dilemma

"Dear Dilemma: Call in a dentist and ask him to examine the mouths of the patients and the dentures, in order to return them to their rightful owners. I am told that denture-marking kits are available. Get one, and use it, before another teeth thief gums up the works again."

Sairey Gamp would have enjoyed the challenge of such a situation. If you do not know Mrs. Sarah Gamp, may I have the joy of introducing her to you? She is one of Charles Dickens' great characters in the novel, "Martin Chuzzlewit." She is a midwife and a general nurse, and her whole life is involved with birth and death. The originality of her language is unparalleled, as she pours out the folklore of what it is like to be poor in the 19th century to all who will listen to her. As she said about her calling, "Bless the babe, and save the mother, is my mortar, sir."

Mrs. Gamp was fat, dumpily clothed, not too young with a somewhat red and swollen nose. She had a face for all occasions, and went to a lying-in or a laying-out with equal zest and relish. She would say to new clients, "Leave the bottle on the chimley-piece, and don't ask me to take none, but let me put my lips to it when I am so dispoged." And as Dickens said, "It was difficult to be in her company without becoming conscious of a smell of spirits." Dickens' irrepressible humor comes out in the things he has Sairey Gamp say, and the *way* she says them.

She had difficulty with the letters "s," "c," and "v." Once she said to a gentleman, "My earnings, sir, is not great, but I will not be impoged upon."

She believed in standing up for others in her "profession," and so one day she recommended her friend, Betsy Prig, for a job of nursing an elderly man who is supposed to be out-of-his-mind. "Betsy Prig has nussed a many lunacies," she tells the client, "and well she knows their ways, which puttin' 'em right close afore the fire, when fractious, is the certainest and most compoging."

Though she is forever flattering her better-off patrons, she never really associates herself with any but the poor. As she says, "Rich folks may ride on camels, but it ain't so easy for 'em to see out a needle's eye. That's my comfort, and I hope I knows it."

Later in the life of Charles Dickens, he gave public readings. They must have been marvelous to hear. He really loved the little people he wrote about. One of his favorites was Mrs. Gamp. Each time he made her come alive on the platform, he would become so amused himself, he never could finish without bursting into laughter and tears.

There is comfort in laughter, not only for those who make others laugh, but also for those who need the healthy release which laughter gives us in the midst of so much that is depressing and sad.

Sarah Gamp lodged on the first-floor-front of a little house, near a mutton-pie shop and directly opposite the cats'-meat warehouse. She was above the barber shop of Mr. Sweedlepipes, who also collected and sold birds. The new clients, particularly of babies about to be born, would rush into the barber shop and demand of Mr. Sweedlepipes where was Mrs. Gamp. One time after he had shouted out to her, she cried impatiently, as she descended the stairs, "Well, what is it? Is the Thames a-fire, and cooking its own fish, Mr. Sweedlepipes?"

There is more to tell about Sairy Gamp, much more, but I will close with another of her observations which she also made to the barber and bird fancier. She said, "We never know wot's hidden in each other's hearts; and if we had glass winders there, we'd need keep the shetters up."

A Time to Ponder: A small explanation needs to be made about the word *perfect*. For example, in Matthew 5:48 it says: "Be ye therefore perfect, even as your Father which is in heaven is perfect." Someone could say,—doesn't perfect mean perfect? I am told that the Greek word "teleios," which is translated "perfect" in the King James' Version, also means "complete," or "mature." Of course, God is perfect, and we as Christians, with the help of the Holy Spirit, are to grow into a maturity of godliness; but never in this world do we attain "sinless perfection." It is a lost cause to champion. One honest look inward explodes the whole theory. We are on firm ground when we hold in mind the truth, no one is perfect.

In the story in First Samuel when one of the sons of Jesse is to be anointed as the future king, Samuel looked at Eliab, the eldest brother of David, and thinks in his heart, "Aha, there is the Lord's anointed." "But the Lord said to Samuel: Pay no attention to his looks or to his splendid height, for I have passed him by. It is not what man sees; for man looks on the outward appearance, but the Lord looks on the heart."

Take time to look up some of the passages in the Bible which tell us what we really are like without Christ and His ever-cleansing blood,—Matthew 15:18-20 and Galatians 5:19 and 20, for example. And then contrast these words with Galatians 5:22, 23.

"There is not one righteous man on earth who does good and never sins. Further, do not pay attention to everything that people say, lest you hear your servant curse you; and you know well enough that in your heart you have cursed others."

I Samuel 16:6, 7   *Matthew 5:48*
Matthew 15:18-20   *Ecclesiastes 7:20-22*
Galatians 5:19-23

34
The Right Balance

It is difficult to maintain a balance in life. If you are too enthusiastic, your critics who do not share your zeal label you a fanatic. And so you try to tiptoe through life being quiet and serene,—you can be certain someone will say that you are lazy, or even worse, lacking in sensitivity. Would that we would learn and remember that no one's perfect, and another great truth: People are different. As an enthusiastic friend of mine says, "Let them be different! That's what makes life colorful."

Yesterday I was watching two children on a teetertotter. They never did have the fun of rocking back and forth, or the added exhilaration of putting their feet up and balancing in the air. Quite the contrary—one timid little girl was always screaming at the top, while her friend and torturer bounced her higher and higher.

It is hard to get the right balance, not only for children, but for all of us, in all areas of living, particularly in what we believe. As one looks back into history, it is easy to find examples of Christians who have not had a healthy balance in their attitude toward music and art. At one time Rembrandt lived among a religious group who took a harsh attitude toward painting. According to their standards, the artist's role was to represent the visible world, and leave the interpretation of the Bible to the theologians. This narrow group felt that an artist had no right to illustrate scenes from the Word of God.

We can be thankful Rembrandt had the courage and good sense to disagree with the unbalanced injunctions. God is not against art and music. Where do these people think creativity came from? But I will hasten to add, all art and music is not for God. There are two main streams in creativity, the constructive and the destructive, and what is confusing, much of what is very beautiful, is in the destructive flow; but that is another subject, and we won't go into it now...

Some years later than Rembrandt, one of the world's greatest composers, Johann Sebastian Bach, found himself in a similar atmosphere of restriction against the arts when he accepted the position of "Cappellmeister" of Cöthen, Germany. All music was banned in the unadorned court chapel, except the singing of psalm tunes. If Bach had been forced to remain in this stifling atmosphere, we most surely would not have the "Saint Matthew Passion" and other matchless compositions which have enriched the souls of people and brought Christian truth, joy and refreshment into lives for well over two hundred years.

Again we are living in a moment when many people, particularly young people, are thirsting for beauty, because they feel dead in the midst of so much artificiality and ugliness. As Christians it should be a constant prayer that God will help us arrive at a wholesome and balanced understanding of how we can worship Him in art, music, literature, and many other ways, so that we might bring back into our lives, our homes, and the world a sense of order and beauty. One way to learn what is genuinely tasteful and beautiful is to study and enjoy the great creators of the past, in order to better understand the present.

In Rembrandt's painting "The Elevation of the Cross" we see a profound conception of humanity, not just a decoration, but a suffering man smitten by God. And the artist put himself at the foot of the cross with his face expressing pain and compassion. It was an extraordinary public confession of what Christ meant to Rembrandt. The Prince of Orange was so pleased when he saw the painting that he ordered the rest of a series of five works. This was one of the few commissions the artist received in his later life.

In his etchings, which he continued to make almost up to the hour of his death, Rembrandt surrounded himself and his Lord with the lame, the poor, the blind, the halt, and the disinherited, who have been and always will be the faithful and beloved companions of the One who came to save "whosoever believeth in Him."

Even though the contemporaries of Rembrandt never knew it (they thought he died a failure), his life came to a logical and right conclusion. Through his frequent reversals and suffering he learned to evaluate success, and therefore was stripped of pretense. When he died, it is true he was still working to pay off debts, and the neighbors, undoubtedly, were still shaking their heads at his "different" life, but what they did not know was that the "unsuccessful" artist had spiritual resources. An unfinished painting of Simeon with the Christ child was found on his easel, and Rembrandt, like Simeon, departed this earth in peace and victory for his eyes beheld the real Christ.

A Time to Ponder: Bach in his lifetime was also plunged into sorrow that a man with little faith would not have been able to survive. When he was still at Cöthen, he was asked one Spring to go with his Prince on a tour which lasted a couple of months. When he left, his wife was in good health and on the day the Prince and his musicians returned to their town, Bach hastened home to be greeted by his beloved family.

He was met at the threshold with the news that his precious wife was already dead and buried. As he stood among his children, stunned, grief-stricken, wondering in a sort of rage, why no one had tried to find him, he looked again. They were only children. How would they know what to do, and he began to take care of them. Out of his sorrow, soon afterwards, he began work again on a chorale that he had put aside. It begins with the words: "God's way is the best way."

Bach could compose music about life and death that moves us deeply, because he was writing out of the experiences of his own life. The drawings and paintings of Rembrandt bring tears to our eyes, because he too had known anguish, loneliness, and misunderstanding. But both of these great men knew where to turn when in need. "Come unto Me, all ye that labour and are heavy laden, and I will give you rest," said the Son of Man. "He healeth the broken in heart, and bindeth up their wounds."

"Humble yourselves therefore under the mighty hand of God, that He may exalt you in due time: Casting all your care upon Him, for He careth for you."

Matthew 11:28
Psalm 147:3
I Peter 5:6, 7

35
Be Generous

"Jim's a good fellow. He'd give you the shirt off his back." I was sitting behind two men on a bus and enjoying one of my favorite indoor sports,—listening to people talk. I suppose it is eavesdropping, but I think of it as "research." A well-known novelist of our age used to ride up and down "the trolley line" copying down scraps of conversation to put in his books. The next time you use public transportation watch what you say. You might end up in a novel or a newspaper column.

Jim's friends had much to say about him. I soon gathered that Jim was not without some faults. He had made a mistake at the shop the day before yesterday. They discussed this awhile, and that reminded them of a few other of his imperfections. These were talked about briefly. Then there was a lull in the conversation, but when they started talking again, one of the men said, "Old Jim's far from perfect, but what a good guy."

The other man agreed, "Yeah, he's got a heart like a tub."

It makes you think of what Peter said: "Above all things have fervent charity among yourselves: for charity shall cover the multitude of sins." It makes you wonder, why are some people more generous than others? Why is it such a hardship for certain persons to give away a handkerchief?

I have noticed that generosity rarely has anything to do with how much people have. It is possible to be big-hearted with a little and stingy with a lot. In passing in review certain people I know who, like Jim, are generous souls, there are two interesting things. One, they had caught their generosity. Most of them had (or have) generous parents, grandparents, and friends. They had lived in an atmosphere of giving, and so giving came naturally. Two, Big-hearted people like other people, and they go one step farther, they believe in their friends. They are not cynical, like Thomas á Kempis, who wrote: "They that today are with you, tomorrow may be against you; and often they turn around like the wind."

A professor I had in college told me the following story: "It was in the depression," he said, "and I was broke—so broke I wasn't sure I was going to be able to feed my family another week. I had an idea for a small business which I was positive was sound, and I needed two hundred dollars to get the thing moving. I went from bank to bank, friend to friend—the minute I mentioned money, everyone stopped listening.

"Then one day Carl came to see me (someone we both knew). 'Hear you need a little help, Phil,' he said. 'Tell me exactly what you have in mind and how much you need.' We talked for hours. Suddenly Carl got to his feet. He looked out the window at his car. He said, 'Think I know where I can get two hundred dollars for that car of mine.' As he went out the door he grinned, 'It's good for a man to walk.' "

One of the rewarding parts about being generous,— these people always seem to have such a good time. They seem free. LeTourneau, the remarkable businessman who has been known for his generous spirit once said, "Not how much of my money do I give to God, but how much of God's money do I keep for myself."

I Peter 4:8

A Time to Ponder: In both the Old and New Testament the teaching is that if you are generous and share what you have with others, you are going to be blessed. God's ways are always the ways of liberality, of flowing over, of bountiful reaping. It is not enough that our generosity should benefit the person in need what an added joy that the one who gives receives also. As it says in Luke, "Give, and it shall be given unto you: good measure, pressed down, and shaken together, and running over, shall men give into your bosom. For with the same measure that ye mete withal it shall be measured to you again." "The liberal soul shall be made fat," says a proverb, "and he that watereth shall be watered also himself." And one more piece of evidence that it is all gain to give: "He which soweth sparingly shall reap also sparingly; and he which soweth bountifully shall reap also bountifully."

Luke 6:38
Proverbs 11:25
II Corinthians 9:6

36
"What Are You Doing Here?"

The philosopher and apostle of pessimism, Arthur Schopenhauer, sat slumped on a park bench in Frankfurt, Germany, deep in dark thoughts. A policeman, mistaking him for a tramp, approached him and said, "Who are you? What are you doing here?"

Schopenhauer replied wearily, "I wish I knew."

It was the early 19th century. The Napoleonic and counter-Napoleonic armies had left scars of ravage all over Europe. Millions of men had perished. Millions of acres of land had been laid waste. Everywhere on the continent life had to begin again at the very bottom. This was the sort of world Schopenhauer was born into, and to add to his troubled state of mind, his father died, apparently by his own hand, when the young man was 17. His mother, a novelist, plunged into a life of "free love." In one of their frequent quarrels, she pushed her son down the stairs. Schopenhauer left home in bitterness, and though his mother lived another twenty-four years, he never saw her again. There were several other things that fed his natural disposition toward pessimism, and then when I read that Schopenhauer lived *in a boarding house* for thirty years,—he had all my sympathy. How could he not be a gloomy person? Have you ever lived in a boarding house?

Again we live in a day when many people wish they too knew what they are doing here on earth. The strained, fast-paced, noisy way of life which has developed in the 20th century has issued in shattered nerves, tangled lives, broken homes, overflowing hospitals, and overworked psychiatrists, psychologists, and counselors.

A minister who spends many hours listening to troubled people said, "We seem to know everything about life except how to live it."

Many years ago, a friend of mine used to sit slumped on a park bench too, across from the Museum of Science and Industry in Chicago. No policeman mistook her for a tramp. She was attractive and well-dressed, but her thoughts were as black as Schopenhauer's.

Whenever I am in Chicago and pass that spot and take a quick look at the bench, I remember what a spiritual battle went on there, and I give thanks to God for the victory that was accomplished in her life. My friend not only found the answer and purpose to life for herself, but she has generously, and with excitement, shared her Saviour with many, many others.

It is right here that a lot of us 20th century Christians have been weak. We are holding in what we are supposed to be giving out. We can be articulate about the latest program on TV, the weather, stocks and bonds, and every last detail of that last trip we took, but when it comes to mentioning the name, Christ, "the hope of the world," we have nothing to say. And many of us

162

have been going in and out of churches since childhood. Does it not seem as if something is lacking?

Not all people are able to talk about their faith, I know this, but we all should be doing something to spread the "good news." Mrs. Charles H. Spurgeon, the wife of the great 19th century preacher, in her lifetime mailed her husband's books to over two hundred thousand people. She was an invalid, and she said once to her husband when they were discussing his latest book, "I wish a copy could be placed with every minister in England."

He said, "Then why not do it?" With a smile, he added, "How much will you give?"

Over the years she had been saving five shilling pieces, and when she promptly brought forth enough money to buy one hundred books, her husband was amazed. And thus began the "Book Fund." Susannah Spurgeon took it seriously, and began to pray that God would move hearts and that people would be led to give money for books.

Inspired by this act of faith, we have made a similar prayer at Chesalet, and with the co-operation of our mothers and many dear friends, we have been privileged to send off thousands of Christian books and records also. This is only a pittance, we realize; but if thousands of other Christians would begin to circulate good literature, we could make some sort of stand against the enemy forces who are flooding the nations with their literature.

Mao Tse-Tung, the head of the Communist party in China, has written a book of poems. It is said that there are more copies of his writings in print than of any other poet in history. He speaks of love, freedom, truth, and human nature, but all in the abstract. The individual in this godless system is of little importance.

Marxism (only another word for communism) is

being taught around the world in the universities, and the great separation between this way of life and true Christianity revolves around you and me. They scorn the individual person. God cares for His people. "The Lord is nigh unto all them that call upon Him, to all that call upon Him in truth."

It is absolutely wrong for us to assume that the people of the world (even those in our own families) know who God is, and what He wants to do for us. I am thankful someone told me that I needed Christ as my Saviour and Lord.

One of the added joys in passing on the gospel message,—you never know when you tell someone about Jesus, how far it will go.

Psalm 145:18

A Time to Ponder: I take John 15:5 seriously, "Without Me you can do nothing." But I also know that there is the part I have to do too. (No one would become a writer if they had not spent the greater part of their time looking around at life, wondering about it, thinking, asking, reading, analyzing, occasionally laughing, but more often, sighing and moaning at much of what has been seen, even suffering a few headaches from the intense concentration; BUT having said all that, it is still *much easier* to write about life than to live it.)

Now back to pondering—If anyone ever asks you for a good definition of the word, Christian, have them turn to Romans 10:9-13. It is so excellent, I think I will put it down right here:

" 'If you confess with your lips the Lord Jesus and believe in your heart that God raised Him from the dead, you will be saved.' For with the heart one believes, so that he is made righteous, and with the mouth confession is made for salvation. For the Scripture says, 'Whoever puts his trust in Him shall not be put to shame.'

"There is then no distinction between Jew and Greek, for they all belong to the same Lord, all-sufficient for all who invoke Him; for 'Everyone who calls on the Lord's name shall be saved.' "

(Berkeley)

To show what fun it is to have "a little project," may I mention a further word about sending out books. As this is definitely a side line with us, we don't do it systematically like Susannah Spurgeon (she even had a special room where they did the packing; we work off the dining room table). But even with the small effort we have made, the Lord has rewarded us. We have heard from people who live in at least fifty countries, from way down under in New Zealand to Alaska. It is very cheering to get letters from India, Sweden, or South Africa on a dreary winter day; and then when one of them tells you that the reader of the book you sent has become a born-again Christian, with this added note: "I am sure you have heard that before, but what makes my situation different is that I have been a minister for ten years." It makes you want to clap your hands for joy and shout your praises to God who wants all men to be saved and come to the knowledge of His truth. No one does anything perfectly, but by the grace of God, let's all press on and do something to show the discouraged of this world that there is hope!

37
More to Follow

A prosperous man left instructions in his will that a certain amount of money was to be given to a minister who had frequently remembered his family with acts of kindness. The widow thought it best to give the money to the pastor in installments rather than one lump sum.

When she mailed the first $25, she placed inside the envelope a piece of paper upon which she had written, "More to follow." Without fail, every two weeks over a period of years, the elderly pastor found an envelope of money in his mailbox with the cheerful message, "More to follow."

The expression, "More to follow," is extra meaningful when recalled in a moment of despondency or despair. It is a deliberate taking hold of a spiritual truth which has been set down for us in Psalm 77. The first nine verses are complaint and unbelief, "Has God forgotten His graciousness? Has His mercy and lovingkindness ceased for all time? Are the promises of God ended?"

Then in verse ten, the turning point comes. The psalmist says, "This is my appointed lot and trial, but I will recall the years of the right hand of the most High. I will remember the works of the Lord."

Instead of allowing his mind to continue turning over and over his troubles and doubts, he now deliberately fixes his whole attention on God. "Surely I will remember Thy wonders of old," he says. "I will meditate also upon all Thy work, and talk of Thy doings."

As the psalmist starts thinking about God, he becomes overwhelmed in his heart, no longer with the greatness of his troubles, but the greatness of the One who is able to help him out of his troubles. You can almost hear him declare, "Who is so great a God as our God? Thou art the God that doest wonders!"

And the same great God will do wonders for us too if we turn outward towards Him instead of inward examining over and over the puny resources we have to withstand in an evil day. We need all of the spiritual strength we can get to meet the dawn with song in this moment in history. As Paul exhorted the Ephesians, "My brethren, be strong in the Lord, and in the power of His might." He was writing for people like ourselves, who had to struggle with the common calamities of human life, and the spiritual battles which have raged in this world and the unseen world since the fall of man. "Put on the whole armour of God," Paul said, "that ye may be able to stand against the wiles of the devil."

Let us not forget that there is always "more to follow" in the Christian life. More protection. More grace. More love. More peace. More forgiveness. More cleansing. More joy. Slip it into a pocket of your mind for the day when you will need it: "More to follow."

Psalm 77
Ephesians 6:10, 11

A Time to Ponder: To have genuine humility before God is not easy for any of us, but when we do bow down and allow the Living Word to work in our stubborn hearts and minds, God's sovereign power helps to solve many of the very problems which have been keeping us from trusting Him. "The Lord is good, a stronghold in the day of trouble; and He knoweth them that trust in Him." "Fear none of those things which thou shalt suffer..." "When He hath tried me, I shall come forth as gold."

Nahum 1:7
Revelation 2:10
Job 23:10

38
Free to Live Cheerfully

What has been said about no one being perfect is meant as encouragement. As I read biographies of those whose names we remember today, it is striking how many of them felt like failures. Years later, sometimes centuries after they struggled, threw away, and tried again, we speak of their works as masterpieces. So let us not be surprised (or quit) because our attempts to express ourselves are not totally satisfying. The main thing is to do something, say something, work on. In the end our painting, poem, or song might prove better than we think; not perfect, but genuine, human, and of value to someone.

An author is always being asked "How do you write a book?" It can be answered simply. Writing comes from having something to say, and then saying it. The "saying it" is the hard part. I am a Beatrix Potter sort of writer which means you scribble some words, strike them out, and write them again and again and again.

Once I had rewritten a column more than seven times, only to return to the first draft and I then simply rearranged it, and put the last paragraph first.

As God's dear children, we do not have to live our lives frantically trying to live up to something beyond us. Doctors tell us that many of our illnesses come from our being so hard on ourselves and critical of others. It sounds odd to say it, but those of us who have accepted Christ as our Saviour are not to make a religion of Christianity. Christ came to set us free. It quickly must be said that this does not mean the freedom to live as we please. It is the contrary.

We are to be followers of the Lord Jesus Christ, who among other things has told us that we are to love our neighbor as ourselves, and that we are to be forgiving people, kind, and merciful; and even more amazing, we are to be of good cheer. Revival will not come to our land until more of us "church" people throw away our homemade religious lists by which we are trying to live, and begin to really live as Christians ought to. "If ye continue in my word," said our Lord, "then are ye my disciples indeed; and ye shall know the truth, and the truth shall make you free." And add to that Paul's liberating words:

"There is therefore now no condemnation to them which are in Christ Jesus, who walk not after the flesh, but after the Spirit." ... "There remain then, faith, hope, love, these three; but the greatest of these is love."

John 8:31, 32
Romans 8:1
I Corinthians 13:13 (Berkeley)

A *Time to Ponder:* Be honest with yourself: If you are being too hard on yourself, ask the Lord to show you how to change a scowl into a smile. Then if you are having a hard time with someone you love very much (or even dislike strenuously), do you think it might be because you are demanding too much from him or her?

There are few people in this imperfect world who can take criticism. It brings out the tiger in us. But it is exciting to see what happens when tigers are given generous servings of kindness, love, and forgiveness.

A neighbor of a friend of mine cut down a tree by mistake which he thought was on his property, but it wasn't. He was prepared for everything from a tongue-lashing to being sued. Instead, my friend when she heard about it simply laughed and said, "I always thought it was an ugly old tree."

By the next afternoon her relieved neighbor and his children arrived at her door with their arms filled with plants. As my friend explained, "They brought enough flowers for a decent burial for two people!"

Pray over Galatians 5:1, 22-26 and 6:1, 2, 7-10.

39
Neighbors

I wonder if there is anybody who has simply added a room to their house? Some friends, who are adding a room, are now also remodeling the kitchen.

"I'm moving the refrigerator to this wall, and the stove will go over there, and ..." the wife was explaining the plan to me as we stood in the "old" kitchen.

"Yes," I interrupted, "but what about the windows?"

She said emphatically, "The carpenter is transferring them to the opposite wall. That side is going to be sealed up."

She explained it this way, as I did look a little puzzled. The neighbor to the west, where the windows are now, is not a lover of small boys, of which my friend has four. She is a chronic complainer, and her countenance is grave and strict. The eastside neighbor always has a smile, even for sooty, little boys who grin up at her as they walk across her flower bed. "The real reason why the windows are being put on the east wall is to make room for the refrigerator on the west wall, but underneath," she grinned, "I'm ornery enough to be glad I won't have to look at that cranky face every time I do dishes from now on!"

I started thinking about certain people I would like to have my windows face, Anna Rose Wright, for instance. She was telling some of us about the experiences she had had when she took a Latvian child into her home.

Andris had lived through the terror of war and being lost and separated from all who were dear to him after the war. These shocks had ripped through his body and soul and left him neither child nor man. He first came into the life of Mrs. Wright when she was teaching in a private school. The other teachers and pupils were shocked when Andris, at lunchtime, grabbed all the food he could get, and then, protecting his "take" with his encircling arms, shoveled things into his mouth.

After the meal, Mrs. Wright simply and kindly explained to Andris that now that he was in America he would have enough to eat. He would no longer have to fight in order to survive. A friendship developed very quickly between the two.

In her book "The Gentle House," Anna Rose Wright tells the story of her adventures in training Andris in the way he should go. He did not last long at the private school, and several months passed while he was shuffled about the country. Everyone said that he was impossible, and moved him on as quickly as they could.

Finally Mrs. Wright paid him a visit. When he saw her, he rushed into her arms. "As I hugged him I said to myself, 'Now don't be an old fool! No! You can't take him home with you! You're too old to tackle a young boy as wild as this one, with your husband dead and gone... It would cramp your style and change your whole way of living. Besides, you can't afford it.' Upon giving myself this sound advice I heard myself say, 'There, there, Andris. Don't cry so hard. Do you want to come home with me?' "

I'd keep all the windows open on that side of my house if Anna Rose Wright lived next door.

A Time to Ponder: There was a cartoon once showing a young mother reclining on the davenport with a pot of coffee at her side; through the window the reader sees her children heading for the school bus. Th expression on the mother's face is choice—a mingled ecstasy, contentment, and great relief. True enough, but don't forget the other end—the teachers, the coaches, the band and orchestra directors, the librarians, the counselors.

The cynic Mencken once wrote, "Man, at his best, remains a sort of one-lunged animal, never completely rounded and perfect, as a cockroach, say, is perfect." True, as I have been trying to say, no human being is perfect, but those who have come through to a way of life that is good and right and wholesome did not fall upon it. They rounded out mainly because somebody believed in them. Someone took time to care for them. There was an exhibition of love shown them.

"For this is the message you have heard from the beginning, that we should love one another... We understand the meaning of love from this, that He laid down his own life on our behalf, and we ought to lay down our lives on behalf of the brothers. Whoever possesses the world's resources and notices that his brother suffers need and then locks his deep sympathies away from him, how is the love of God lodging in him?

"Dear children, let us not be loving in word and tongue, but in deed and truth."

I John 3:11, 16-18 (Berkeley)

174

40
These Little Troubles

Yesterday a letter came from a friend who was told a few months ago that she has an incurable disease. Her letter had a calm, comforted sound, as she reported several small but significant evidences that God is aware that she needs help in this difficult moment.

Unexpectedly, two days before she went to the hospital, her parents arrived and took over the running of her home. After they left, some members from her church supplied meals and formed work crews to help keep the house orderly and clean. In trying to thank these friends, the only response she received was, "It is our joy to help in any way possible."

Then later when she was better, but not really well, she began to feel sad because her illness had caused her children and husband to lose the joy of a summer vacation. She prayed quietly about it, and then at a church meeting a couple gave her husband the keys to an apartment in the beautiful mountains of Colorado, where the entire family had one of the most refreshing holidays they had ever experienced. As she wrote, "It was a superb family vacation to remember for life!"

There is something in all of us which hates to be sidetracked because of illness, broken bones, the debility which we have to struggle against as we add years to our present age, and many other such assorted miseries which make their appearances in the adventure known as living. An elderly lady badly crippled with arthritis once asked her minister,

"Robertson, why does God let us get old and weak? Why must I hurt so?" And it is not only older people who hurt,—for some it begins in childhood. He answered it this way:

"I'm not sure, but I have a theory. I think God has planned the strength and beauty of youth to be physical. But the strength and beauty of age is spiritual. We gradually lose the strength and beauty that is temporary so we'll be sure to concentrate on the strength and beauty which is forever."

There is truth in what the minister said, but why limit ourselves to theory when we have the flaming truth of God to help us walk on a rocky path when the mist hides the way. "The outward man does indeed suffer wear and tear," said Paul, "but every day the inward man receives fresh strength. ('Our light affliction,' or as Phillips translated it)—These little troubles, which are really so transitory, are winning for us a permanent, glorious and solid reward out of all proportion to our pain. For we are looking all the time not at the visible things but at the invisible. The visible things are transitory: it is the invisible things that are really permanent."

A Time to Ponder: Thomas Morley, a sixteenth century musician, in writing to a friend explained that his health had been so bad that he would have been content to have "Him who makes all things, take him out of the world." But later the composer realized that because of his illness he was compelled to stay at home, and in the long, solitary hours he had to do something to fill up the time; and so he wrote some songs. Very little original music for the plays of Shakespeare has survived, and Morley composed one if not two of these songs.

Often, the only way illness and suffering can be rightly understood is afterwards. Paul in telling of some of the perplexing and puzzling things he experienced in his life, commented, "All this is for your benefit, so that the grace that is reaching more and more people may cause thanksgiving to overflow to the glory of God. Therefore we do not lose heart."

You know as well as I do that I could fill the pages of this book with accounts of those who have, and are experiencing that many are the afflictions of the righteous, but the Lord delivers those who trust Him out of them all. It is well to read Psalm 34 on a dreary day.

If Bernard of Clairvaux had been a robust young man, we would not have the beloved hymn, "O Sacred Head Now Wounded," but because of poor health he was unfit for military service, and early destined for the church. There he truly centered his life in God and Christ, and from his frail but dedicated body flowed creativity, wisdom, and good sense which has enriched the life of the whole Church from his day to ours.

"Dear Lord, Keep us from losing heart when the days seem extra long. How thankful we are for Your mercy and lovingkindness when illness makes us troubled and weary. May we see our lives in the right perspective, and know that our light afflictions (these little troubles) which seem so heavy now will soon be over for all who trust You, and the joys to come will last

41
A Noble Cause

Here in the Swiss Alps, along with a few other concerns, we are involved in a small, cheerful, and profitable adventure: the raising of chickens in the woodshed behind our chalet. I presume to say "we," because the musician friend who lives with me takes care of the chickens, and I eat the eggs.

While cleaning out the small shed in preparation for the new feathered inmates (a task which probably had not been accomplished in a couple of hundred years, as the small renovated barn in which we live was built in 1711), we were thankful for the help of a dear friend who had come to Switzerland from South America to be "spiritually refreshed." There are times in life when there is nothing like hard, physical work to prepare the soul for spiritual renewal.

Even before the chickens were driven up the winding road in the backseat of our old car and established in their new home, we had decided to call it The Golden Egg Inn. This was not a name chosen hastily as these hens were destined to participate in a noble cause, as the whole point in having chickens at the beginning was to sell eggs to help buy a Flentrop organ for the L'Abri chapel.

Now years have gone by, the organ long since paid for, and we still have chickens,—a fresh, energetic, new crew every two years. There are several reasons why chickens are favored in this house. I ask you— have you ever heard a hen cackle after she has laid an egg? It is one of the most cheerful, hilarious sounds I know. It is difficult to be depressed when chickens are near. And then what can be tastier than a really cackling-fresh egg? We are also thankful for eggs as a meat substitute.

One day when the musician came in from watering, feeding, talking, and singing to her chickens she told me that in her opinion the trouble with America is that people don't have chickens anymore. And now that I have had time to consider the statement, the more certain I am that she is right. It *is* undoubtedly what is wrong with Australia, England, and other countries.

The proposition could be restated in these words: "The trouble with the world today is that many people have lost their sense of wonder, appreciation, and thankfulness to God for what He has given to mankind." It is easy in our fast-paced, impersonal world to become unappreciative, stale, and lacking in wonder as we slide (like on a conveyer belt) from one day to the next, not taking time to marvel at chickens, for an example.

One of our neighbors said recently, "Having chickens is a dead loss," and in his case it is. Out of a dozen hens they get an egg or two a week. But the ten Golden Egg Inn residents often have ten eggs a day, except in the molting season (even chickens need a vacation). As

the Inn director says, "Make them lay and they will pay." Music is important to chickens, as well as lots of fresh water, grain, grit, all the leftovers from the table (chickens are the most effective garbage disposal I have seen, and much cheaper), and they love fresh greens from the garden.

It is not "our" theory that chickens respond to music. In Dunn, North Carolina, one of the radio stations devotes part of its evening time to "Music for Chickens." The farmers in the region say that the station music which is piped into hen houses and barns helps to make chickens lay more eggs, and it also soothes the cows.

A Time to Ponder: In January because of snow on the steep road in back of our chalet on our return to Switzerland after 44 days in the U.S.A., I deposited the singer and our luggage in a snow bank and drove off to find a place to park the car. In the meantime, a friend trudging up the path saw us unload the suitcases and groceries and said that she would go and get help. While the musician was waiting, she began to call Owl, our cat. As she was singing out, "Owlie, OWLIE!!" suddenly, below in the woodshed there was a great commotion,—loud clucking, cackling, and excited flapping of wings. The Golden Egg Inn chickens had recognized the singer's voice and were telling each other, "Cluckety-cluck, cluckety-cluck, she's back! *she's back!* cackle, cackle, cackle!" ...

If chickens, which the *World Book* scurrilously speaks of as "not very intelligent," can recognize the voice of their caretaker, what confidence it should give us, who are spoken of as made in God's image, to call upon Him in our every need.

> "What is man, that Thou art mindful of him? ...
> Thou madest him to have dominion over the works of Thy hands ... the beasts of the field; the fowl of the air ...
> O LORD, our Lord, how excellent is Thy name in all the earth!"   *Psalm 8:4, 6, 7-9*

182

42
Make No Hasty Conclusions

As anyone knows who lives near a lake or by the sea, a storm can arise quickly. At the end of the 16th century a fisherman was standing on a cliff on one of the Orkney Islands north of Scotland, and in a state of shock he watched a storm batter his cottage, his boat, and fishing tackle. The man was a Christian, but as he witnessed the destruction of all he possessed, his thoughts were as black and swirling as the sky.

But little did he know that this very same storm had sunk part of the Spanish Armada, and not only had spared England the terror of a Spanish Inquisition with its torture and death, but it would have certainly stifled The Elizabethan Age, which was one of the heroic, rich moments in the history of English-speaking people. To mention only a few great names whose influence is still felt today:—Shakespeare, John Donne, Francis Bacon, Ben Jonson, Christopher Marlowe, and John Webster; and, of course, the climaxing and culminating literary achievement in 1611 was the King James Version of the Bible.

At any given moment in life, we do not see all that is happening. That is why God tells us to wait, be patient, do not come to hasty conclusions.

Another example of one who might have thought his prayers were not answered, and who certainly could have ended with bitterness and resentment in his heart was the great American missionary, Adoniram Judson. On his deathbed he heard that some Jews in Turkey had come to believe in Christ as their Saviour through reading about his sufferings while preaching the gospel in Burma. In awe Judson told a friend, "As a young man I prayed that I might go to Jerusalem because I had a deep concern for Jewish people; but instead the Lord sent me to Burma, and to suffer torture in Burmese prisons. Now in this extraordinary way God has brought some Jews to repentance in Turkey."

Even though the Spirit is able to move on wings of wind, there are times when all that God's people can do is to wait; but we can learn from those in the past who have waited upon the Lord that God does not forget His people. Joseph is one of the few men in history about whom we do not have to say: "He was a great man, but ..." We remember with thanksgiving the godly character of Joseph, and his wisdom, kindness, good sense, and his nobility of spirit which had no room for resentment. He called one of his sons Ephraim, which means fruitful, because, he said, "God hath caused me to be fruitful in the land of my affliction."

A Time to Ponder: When Fanny Crosby was six weeks old, a slight cold caused an inflammation in her eyes. The family physician was called, but he not being at home, a stranger came in his place. He recommended the use of hot poultices, which tragically resulted in the loss of her sight. When the sad event became known throughout her neighborhood, the man left town, and no one in the community ever heard from him again. What is remarkable is to hear that Fanny Crosby said concerning this tragedy. "In more than 85 years," she said, "I have not for a moment felt a spark of resentment against him, for I have always believed from my youth up that the good Lord, in His infinite mercy, by this means consecrated me to the work that I am still permitted to do."

I for one am thankful for the hymns of Fanny Crosby, particularly, "Near the Cross," "Blessed Assurance," and "Praise Him! Praise Him!"

If you are bewildered at this moment because of some inexplicable sorrow, hold in mind that God will fulfill His purpose in your life in His timing and in His way. It will be as certain with you as it was with Job. "He knows the way I take," said Job. "When He has tried me, I shall come forth as gold."

43
Faith Must Show

A father was preparing a Sunday School lesson one Saturday afternoon. His young son came running across the family room on his way outside to play. As the boy reached the door, the father called out, "Wait, hold it—I want to talk to you."

The youngster stood poised at the door ready to leap out the second his parent was through talking.

"No, no," said the father, motioning to the couch. "Come here and sit down. I need an audience."

It had occurred to the young father (who was for the first time in his life teaching a Sunday School class while the regular teacher was away for a vacation) that it was unreasonable for him to spend time teaching the children of other couples and not make an attempt to get across some of the same material to his child.

The boy dragged back into the room with a sour look on his face and reluctantly dropped down on the floor near the couch.

The father said good-naturedly, "Come on, Bill, be a good sport. I'm not going to take your whole afternoon. I'll even drive you to the skating rink if you'll give me fifteen minutes of your time."

The captive audience was not the least interested the first few minutes, but the teacher went on, hoping to get the attention of his son. Several of the books he had been studying in the Bible had become vivid to him, and the book of James particularly fascinated him. What he was trying to do was put into simple language a description of a Christian using examples from the Bible, and then relating it to what a Christian should be like today.

Sometimes when teaching children, you cannot tell by watching the faces and the squirming bodies how much is being absorbed, but he had the satisfaction of knowing that Bill seemed to be listening. He was frowning and pulling at his cheek, definite symptoms that the boy was concentrating.

At last the lesson was over, and he was told that he was free to go and play, but instead of jumping up, Bill continued to sit with his back against the wall and his chin dropped into his hands.

"Something bothering you, Bill?"

"No," he said as he started to zip up his jacket, "not exactly." Then in that innocent way children have which often leave us adults open-mouthed and speechless, he added, "But I was just wondering, Dad, if I've ever seen a Christian."

Having said that, he jumped to his feet, skipped across the room and shouted cheerfully as he slammed the door. "Bye, I'll be back in ten minutes so you can take us skating."

A Time to Ponder: In England in the days before the Welfare State, a poor farmer with a large family was laid up for a time with a broken leg. The members of his church called a special meeting to pray for their friend. One after another the members prayed that God would help the unfortunate family and provide their needs. In the midst of the prayer meeting there was a loud knock at the door. Outside stood the son of another member of the village church. With his hat in his hands, he announced shyly to the person who opened the door, "My Dad could not attend the prayer meetin' tonight, so he sent his prayers in a wagon." And there was the wagon, loaded with pumpkins and potatoes, meat, fruit, eggs, and many other products from the farm.

Brief prayer for parents, aunts and uncles, and grandparents: "Dear Lord, Remind us that often what we do in life speaks louder than what we say. May the world know we are in it by the good works we accomplish, not giving credit to ourselves, but to our God and Saviour Whom we worship. May the children of our generation see a few more Christians. Thank You, and we pray in the name of the Lord Jesus Christ. Amen."

"... It isn't enough just to have faith. You must also do good to prove that you have it. Faith that doesn't show itself by good works is no faith at all—it is dead and useless."

Iames 2:17 (The Living Bible)

44
Go On!

Many years ago when I lived on the edge of Lake Minnetonka in Minnesota, I attended (off and on) the Christian Writers' club which met once a month in Minneapolis. Part of the idea was that it is better to laugh together than cry alone. We were encouraged to bring our unpublished manuscripts of which most of us had drawers-full. Some of these were read outloud, and we would give each other ideas how they could be improved (it is *always* easier to see the weaknesses in others' manuscripts than in your own). Quite a few of our unpublished manuscripts simply needed to be thrown into a wastebasket and thought of as disciplining and training for the next poem, article, or book we hoped to write.

Then we would share things we had read or heard which had "inspired" us since the last time we met together. I remember a minister in our group. His dream was to write a novel. He told us about Laurence Sterne, another minister turned novelist. He said that Sterne's fame rests on one unfinished novel, "The Life and Opinions of Tristram Shandy." "Even if Sterne had lived to be 100," said our minister, "he would undoubtedly not have finished his novel, because in Volume Nine, Shandy is still a baby!" He added with a smile, "So you see, the main thing is to get started."

Not only were these hours together helpful in the way of improving our technique, but it was morale-lifting to know that you were not the only writer in Minnesota collecting letters which began: "Thank you for allowing us to see the enclosed material. Unfortunately, we are unable to use it, but we appreciate your submitting it for our consideration."

These depressing and miserable form letters are known in the writing profession as "rejection slips." Writers use the backsides of them for shopping lists or to write further material for rejection, to paper the walls, to line drawers, and to wrap up garbage. What is extra damaging is that a new writer does not have an overflow of confidence, and then to have nearly everything you mail out sent back to you with *one of those* letters is depressing. But the main thing, we keep telling ourselves, is to go on. Don't give up. Be fervent in spirit, serving the Lord.

Then there would be an occasional exhilarating evening when one in our midst would swagger into a meeting with a letter of acceptance from an editor and a check for five or ten dollars included. We would all be as proud and happy at this event as though it had happened to each one of us.

We had good times together in our writer's club in Minneapolis enjoying those infrequent triumphs, but the most important part was the "camaraderie" and the encouraging of each other to try again. To go on.

A Time to Ponder: "If there is something you have bungled terribly, let that be and go on," said a former missionary, "But don't be cumbered by something

Wake up, O harp and lyre!
we will meet the dawn with song.
Psalm 108:2

you've done well either. 'Forget the things that are behind' and 'press on.' "

One summer I attended a poetry seminar. Our professor said that it is the function of the poet to make the
commonplace come alive. His goal should be to make
the reader feel that he has been blind, and now he sees.

"If there is anything I can't stand," he said, "it's security!"

Too often we cling to the security of where we are, and what we have done. If we do strike out and do something new and exciting, there will be those "what-will-people-say?" taskmasters, of course. Mrs. Peter Matson, whom I quoted above, had a long row of eyebrows raised at her when she decided to go to the mission field. She was over thirty, unmarried, a business woman, and a fashionable dresser.

But she made it to China, all right, and a wonderful missionary she was, because she was doing what God had placed in her heart to do. There is an added note of victory to the story: One of the board members in particular was very opposed to having an older, "worldly" woman in *their* mission field. He later became her husband! Press on. Don't give up. Away with complaining. Do something different. You never know what might happen! Don't wait for perfect conditions, or a perfect you, or perfect other people. That is reserved for the better land to which we are going if we trust and believe in the Lord Jesus Christ.

Even today, "this one thing I do, forgetting those things which are behind, and reaching forth unto those things which are before, I press toward the mark for the prize of the high calling of God in Christ Jesus."

Philippians 3:13, 14

"Not that I have already made this my own or have already reached perfection, but I am pressing onward."

Philippians 3:12

"May the God of your hope so fill you with all joy and peace in believing—through the experience of your faith—that by the power of the Holy Spirit you may abound and be overflowing (bubbling over) with hope."

Romans 15:13 (Amplified)